Isna Gabriel Sia

Dances of the Brasa (Balanta) People of Guinea-Bissau in Contemporary Times

Isna Gabriel Sia

Dances of the Brasa (Balanta) People of Guinea-Bissau in Contemporary Times

Kussunde, Kanta Po and Broska

ScienciaScripts

Imprint

Cover image: www.ingimage.com

This book is a translation from the original published under ISBN 978-620-2-03834-8.

Publisher:
Sciencia Scripts
is a trademark of
Dodo Books Indian Ocean Ltd. and OmniScriptum S.R.L publishing group

120 High Road, East Finchley, London, N2 9ED, United Kingdom
Str. Armeneasca 28/1, office 1, Chisinau MD-2012, Republic of Moldova, Europe
Managing Directors: Ieva Konstantinova, Victoria Ursu
info@omniscriptum.com

Printed at: see last page
ISBN: 978-620-8-40101-6

I dedicate this work to all the students and friends at Unilab who have worked so hard to develop the university. To my parents, N'ghate Namara (Gabriel Sia) and M'pabi M'bunda, who effectively invested what they had in my studies, sometimes sacrificing part of the family to fund and contribute to my education. To my family, especially my cousin Santa Namara, to the members of the Ebenezer Evangelical Christian Church and, finally, to all my friends, particularly: Luis Cumba, Ibra Co, Justino Iala, Paulo Sergio de Proenga, Virginio Mendes, Julio Machado, Dona Luiza, Caroline R. Cardoso, Noe Vitorino V. Co, Babek da Silva, Alves lanta, Domingos Mendonga, Pinto Chico Nancassa, Edvaldo Nunes Oddair Correia, Augusto Imbali Infanda, Francisco Cumba, Constantino Domingos Gomes, Rosilda Santiago, Jorgito Cusna, Rubem Imbana, Jeremias Demba, Rocio Contento, Sabino Tobana, Paulo Batica, Naentrem Sanca, Luis Fernandes Junior, Silas Intchama, Roberto Gongalves, Almeida Djata, Wasca Djata, Dabana Naualna, Tino Injai, Hipolito Mendes, Alfredo Luis Camara, Costa Menu, Rafael Joao Malaca, Fabricio Sena, Gerhard Seibert, Abna Nhanque, Benjamim Fiere, Vladimir Renato Nanfadi, Ivo Aloide Ie, Julio Agostinho Digna (Juadi), Emanuel de Jesus Nhaga, Joselito Crispim, Beto Infande, Emilio Mario Te (Midana), Orlando Ca, Tony Costa, Vavito Andre da Costa, Joao Eusebio Imbatene, Valdir Bicale, Vinicius da Silva, Eduardo Estevam, Fabio Baqueiro, Bitentua Fiere, Gloria Augusto Ca, Julio Quintino Cam-nate Sumba, Anderson Cafe and Adelmaria Ione dos Santos for having supported me directly and indirectly.

ACKNOWLEDGMENTS

To my God, for giving me the gift of this earthly life; to my parents, for the support and courage they gave me in this very difficult endeavor.

I would like to thank my family, friends, technical administrators and teachers at Unilab, as well as all the employees and collaborators who work at the same institution, especially my magnificent advisor Prof. Dr. Gerhard Seibert for his patience, sincerity and encouragement during the course of this work.

I would like to thank my dear Judite Yufa, who calls me from time to time to show her concern and complacency; I will always be grateful to her.

I would like to thank the people who gave me interviews for my ethnographic research in both Guinea-Bissau and Brazil, namely: Carlitos Quime Namara, Ze Augusto Nhaga, Santa Namara, Pedro Quinda, Sangasson Namara, Isnaba Intchala, Duarte Sanha, Dinis Quade, Alberto Bedam, Pansau Nayette, N'ghate Namara, Wiltik Na Brenha, Jose Fundo Tempo, among others.

I would like to thank the government of Luis Inacio Lula da Silva for having created a distinguished university like Unilab, which, in effect, integrates Brazil with the Portuguese-speaking African countries and East Timor.

It has been a pleasure and an honor to be a student at this institution, because Unilab has made me start to think differently about Africa and black people; my view of the world is undergoing transformations every day, despite the fact that I am a beginner in academic life and do not yet have a broad view when it comes to analyzing world situations.

As a student at Unilab, I've noticed that the syllabus studied in my country is markedly Eurocentric, as it talks specifically about the history of the first and second world wars, the crisis of the 1929s, the industrial revolution and the French revolution, the Spanish civil war, among other historical events in Europe. As for African subjects, only the history of a few empires is studied, namely: Mali, Songai and Ghana. We also study very little about African leaders. With regard to our charismatic leader Amilcar Lopes Cabral, I always heard about him from teachers, people in the street and on the radio; however, we never talked about him in the school syllabus. After joining Unilab, I began to study and learn about the life and work of great African, Afro-Brazilian and Middle Eastern visionary leaders and thinkers, such as Kwame N'krumah, Ki-Zerbo, Cheik Anta Diop, Sedar Senghor, Du Bois, Malcon X, Martin Luter King, Milton Santos, Edward Said, among others.

In addition, we studied some of the contents of the eight-volume *General History of Africa,* which is a masterpiece for the historiography of the continent; finally, we also studied *Black Africa - History and Civilizations,* by Elikia M'bokolo, (Volume I and II), among other titles.

Unilab was created to promote cooperation between Brazil and Portuguese-speaking African countries, including East Timor, and, by extension, to value blacks, Indians and historically marginalized people. It is worth noting that some people, even if they are part of it, are still unable to see the reality that we have been experiencing since ancient times.

It is our duty to applaud with great enthusiasm the initiative of Luis Inacio Lula da Silva's government to create a university of international integration, because it has allowed us to deal with people from different countries of the Community of Portuguese Speaking Countries (CPLP); this, in fact, makes us aware of the multiplicity of cultures and customs of these countries, which is very important for further strengthening cooperation at all levels. This knowledge will serve as a foundation in the future, should one of us take up a relevant post in our country of origin, in order to facilitate cooperation in different areas.

Unilab challenges us, when we return, to change the syllabuses of our countries' education systems, making room for more in-depth study of the African continent, particularly the study of our country's history, which is hardly studied at all in schools, both private and public.

From these studies, we will be able to promote and praise our continent, which is coveted, albeit in a veiled way, by Europeans, Americans, Chinese and Indians, who do not want to exploit our natural resources for the economic development of their countries.

Unilab is therefore doing something significant in the lives of each of us, so we should take advantage of these opportunities to continue our studies on the African continent, so that we can deconstruct and demystify the negative view of Africa in general.

Terms like "dance" cannot simply be transferred from Western languages and concepts to the languages and concepts of different cultures and movement systems. Specific cultural values must be taken into account and applied to a specific set of cultural forms in a specific society. Understanding how these terms can be applied depends on a general understanding of the way of life and the systematic relationships between cultural forms and social actions to which they relate. The "cultural form" we call "dance" is far from a universal concept. "Dance", or structured systems of movement, may be universal, but dance is not a universal language.

(KAEPPLER, 2013, p. 88-89).

PRESENTATION

This beautiful book by Isna Gabriel Sia, beautifully written with the pen of commitment and the ink of proclamation, has strong links with his people, his land, his culture, in all its richest and most captivating aspects. A Guinean studying in Brazil, the author is living a temporary exile that brings him closer than it distances him from his land and his people. As a result, he has the advantage of being able to look at his people, his origins and himself with a methodologically distanced and critical eye, although no less passionate and proud; far from his eyes, close to his heart.

There are no better cultures than others; there are different cultures. If it weren't for a conviction that has already been formed and established, that would be a necessary conclusion from reading this book. It is important to note that there is little bibliography on the subject; the few titles that do exist do not always escape the temptation to direct suspicious - if not prejudiced - glances at the presentation and characterization of African cultural manifestations.

Dangas, like other cultural manifestations, say a lot about the dynamic organization of a people, especially in terms of the anthropological dimension. As cultures change, they change over time and space.

This is what the young researcher Isnany Namara is concerned with. He has set out to understand and record the form and content of three dangas from the Brasa ethnic group in Guinea-Bissau. The dangas depicted are *Broska, Kanta Po* and *Kussunde,* from the Brasa (Balanta) ethnic group.

The *Broska* dance takes place at significant moments in community life and serves to create and maintain bonds of fraternity and social cohesion, especially among young people. Performances of this dance take place to promote competition between *tabankas* (villages): the emulation is not predatory, but epic; it represents the permanent challenge of human beings to overcome contingencies - of nature, of history, of their biopsychological limitations - in the inevitable challenge of giving meaning and purpose to the seductive and perverse mystery of living.

When the *Kanta Po* dance takes place, the local competitors provide food and drink for the participants from other places; it is also a dance in which emulation is present; supernatural powers are invoked to achieve victory; winning is important not only for the participants, but for the village they represent, with the consequences of recognition and distinction.

The *Kussunde* dance is a celebration. It takes place when there is an overabundance of rice; it is thus linked to the cycles of nature, which represents the perpetuation of human life in its symbiotic relationship with our Mother Earth. It is also a sign of gratitude and recognition. The *Kussunde* dance takes place all over Guinea.

These dangas are cultural recurrences, linked to so many other similar manifestations, near and far; they combine complex cultural elements, in addition to the playful aspect: festivals, music, movement, drum sounds, meals - all give shape to a scenario of cosmic drama; these representations contribute to the cohesion of the group and to a teleological movement that guides personal and social life, through a relationship of belonging to a group and to nature and links with divine powers, all sustained in a local and universal mythical dimension, in communion with what human creations produce that is most enlightening and enigmatic.

Thus, these dangas synthesize the saga of a people and the reference values that distinguish them, despite the changes they undergo for various and sometimes unavoidable reasons.

The result of Isna Sia's book is a challenge to overcome the Europeanized, biased, supposedly superior gaze; one can perceive in the dangas described in this book a genuine pulse of life that tugs at the strings of hope for a utopian world in which cultures have the right to be what they simply are: manifestations of the human spirit, in eloquent testimonies of epic greatness and dignity.

Sao Francisco do Conde-BA (Brazil), November 03, 2017.

Paulo Sërgio de Proenga

PhD in Letters from the University of São Paulo (USP), professor of Letters at the University of the International Integration of Afro-Brazilian Lusophony - Unilab-BA, Campus dos Males.

SUMMARY

1 INTRODUCED

This paper deals with a topic that is little covered in academia by anthropologists interested in studying and learning about the cultural identity of the Brasa people. I hope that this paper will serve to disseminate the fact that, for the Brasa, although some have abandoned these dances, they are very important in both religious and social life, since "like music, dance is part of a people's cultural heritage. It is a powerful vector of ethnic, sexual, age and social hierarchical identity. Like music, dance can be understood from multiple perspectives." (ZEMP, 2013, p. 31).

This work seeks to portray the dangas of the Brasa people in contemporary times and also to analyze the impact and influence they have suffered in the face of changes in some socio-cultural elements that may be losing their original characteristics; it also seeks to analyze the dynamics and impacts of these dangas on contemporary Brasa society and to describe the original elements of the dangas that have undergone mutations; finally, it seeks to study the characteristics that have remained in the cultural identity of the dangas of this community in the context of contemporary times.

In addition, the research question is as follows: to what extent has the identity of the Brasa people, manifested through the dangas *(Kussunde, Kanta Po* and *Broska),* changed in the face of the external influences to which the community has been subjected?

From my experience in the Brasa community, I realize that every day some cultural characteristics are changing. This may be due to external influences from other cultures. Faced with this situation, I notice that some practices are falling into disuse and others are remaining, because the Brasa (Balanta) are being influenced by other cultures. This is effectively bringing many innovations within the Brasa to the detriment of original elements of the dangas.

This work is considered to be of the utmost importance, as it deals with some elements of the dangas that are losing their functions in contemporary times. It is also about analyzing the way they are seen within the Brasa. It is clear that these external influences contribute to the improvement of elements of the dangas and in some of the cultural manifestations of the same people.

Furthermore, I noticed that very few authors have written about the culture of the Brasa and their writings focus on political, social and religious organization, but I haven't seen any written works about the dangas. For this reason, I thought it would be good to write about these cultural aspects, a topic of great importance, so that people who don't belong to this culture could get to know it more closely and thus take an interest in it and spread it around the world.

The methodology used was based on anthropological research and bibliographical research. As a data collection technique, I used semi-structured interviews, as well as research on internet sites, publications (books, articles), and audiovisual material (videos, images, etc.). In addition, with regard to the cultural manifestations of the Brasa, this is the fruit of the ethnographic research that I began during my stay in GuiC-Bissau before coming to Brazil, and which I have now been able to complete.

The subjects of my research are dangarinos and Brasa danga sympathizers. I also did this work via video call and questions asked via the internet (Facebook), as well as telephone contact with my uncle and cousins who are here in Brazil, asking them questions about elements relating to my research subject. These were pre-defined questions, based on key themes. However, face-to-face interviews were also carried out in Sao Paulo and Rio de Janeiro. In this city, I was able to interview my cousin Carlitos, from whom I obtained some information that certainly helped me structure and enrich my work. I also interviewed some people in Portugal over the internet. I had the help of my colleague Cristiano Quel Side and my cousin Augusto Imbali Infanda, who live in GuiC-Bissau and helped me a lot by interviewing people who are there. In the course of this research, I also analyze the videos and images I already have with me and those I watch on the internet, all of which depict these dangas. In short, I've already interviewed sixteen people at random, apart from those that my cousin Augusto Imbali Infanda and my friend Cristiano Quel Side interviewed in Bissau.

This work is structured in four main chapters, in addition to the introduction and final considerations. I have also compiled a glossary of technical terms, explaining some of the specific terms used throughout this research. In the first chapter, I discuss the contextualization and historical panorama of GuiC-Bissau, portraying the geographical situation of the country; from a historical point of view, I discuss: the arrival of the Portuguese; the three myths of Portuguese colonization in the 1960s (Castro Henriques); the founding of the PAIGC (African Party for the Independence of Guinea-Bissau and Cape Verde); the national liberation war; Guinea-Bissau's independence and the post-independence period. More specifically, I deal with the identity of the Brasa people and the emergence of the name Balanta, the socio-political organization of the Brasa, the composition of names, the stages of formation of both men and women, and the economy, centred on rice cultivation.

The second chapter deals with the concept of *Kussunde* and its purpose, as well as the *Kussunde* dance, which is performed when there is an overabundance of rice, as a sign of gratitude and recognition of the achievements of the *Iras (Buule)* and the ancestors. I also discuss the characteristics of the three groups that make up this dance, namely: *nghaies, dany kussunde, n'guatch* commonly known as *m'pebe.* The chapter ends with reflections on the changes that have taken place in *Kussunde.*

The third chapter looks at *Kanta Po* and first deals with the etymology of the concept of *Kanta Po* and its conceptual shift to Brasa culture. In addition, it shows that *Kanta Po* is a very essential element in consonance with the profane and the sacred, because the dangarinos are linked to the Iras who, in effect, help them in the clashes, that is, in the disputes they carry out in order to win the dance. Throughout the chapter, we tried to characterize the dance and its participants, pointing out that the disputes are much more symbolic than material. The chapter ends with reflections on the changes that took place at *Kanta Po.*

The fourth chapter deals with the definition and creation of the *Broska* dance in the context of Brasa culture, depicting that the *Broska* is celebrated with the aim of socializing and strengthening friendships and social cohesion among Brasa youth. In the course of the description, the characteristics of the *Broska* dance and its participants were shown, as well as the symbolic elements that are at play and the purpose of this dance for the Brasa culture. It ends with reflections on the changes that have taken place in the *Broska* dance within Brasa culture.

2 BRIEF CONTEXTUALIZATION AND HISTORICAL OVERVIEW OF GUINEA BISSAU

Figure 1 - Political map of Guind-Bissau

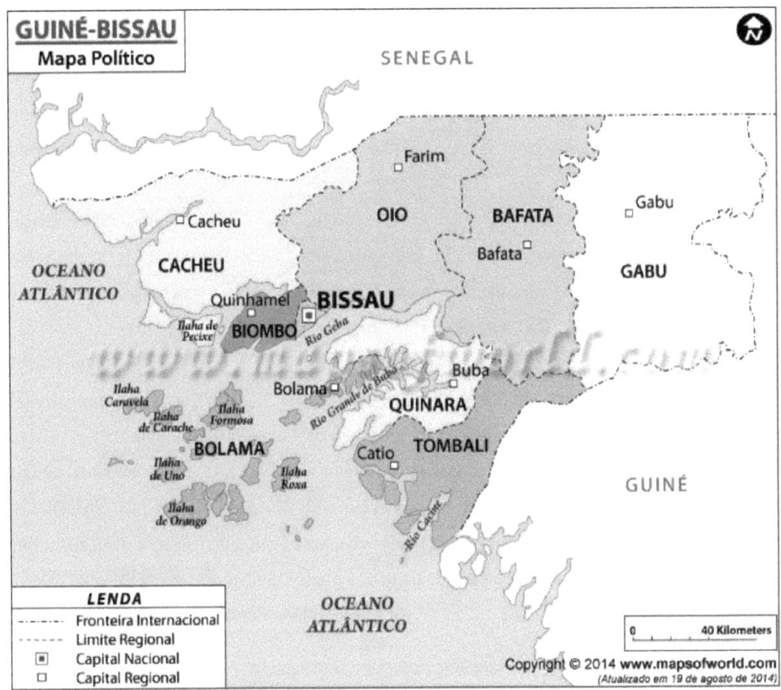

Source: Maps of the World (Aug. 19, 2014).[1]

The Republic of Guind-Bissau is located on the West Coast of Africa, has an area of 36,125 km[12] and a population of 1,530,673 (2015 census)[2] . It is bordered to the north by Senegal and to the south and east by Guind-Conacry, and to the west by the Atlantic Ocean. It has a tropical climate and is a flat country with more than 80 islands and islets, mostly inhabited by Bijagos. Guind-Bissau has two seasons: rainy and dry. The rainy season begins on May 15 and ends on November 15, while the dry season begins on November 15 and ends on May 15.

Administratively, Guinea-Bissau is divided into eight regions, namely: Bafata, Biombo,

[1] Available: <http://pt.mapsofworld.com/guinea-bissau/>. Accessed on: October 29, 2016.
[2] Available:<http://www.stat-guinebissau.com/>. Accessed on: September 3, 2016.

Bolama/Bijagos, Cacheu, Gabu, Oio, Quinara and Tombali, in addition to the Autonomous Sector of Bissau, the capital (SAB). The regions are divided into sectors, which in turn are divided into headquarters. The regions are presided over by governors and both the sectors and the secedes are presided over by administrators. All are chosen by the government.

Despite its small size, Guinea-Bissau has a great cultural diversity, as it is a multi-ethnic country, with the following peoples within its territory: Balanta (Brasa), Fula, Manjaku, Papel, Mandinga, Mankanha, Felupe, Beafada, among others. It is important to note that some of Guinea-Bissau's peoples have been absorbed by others, such as the Nalu, Padjadinga, Djakanka and others.

The current borders were defined 130 years ago, since "What is now Guinea-Bissau corresponds exactly to the territory of the then province of Guinea, resulting from the Luso-French Convention of 1886 and the successive border adjustments, which ended in the first decade of the 20th century." (SILVA; SANTOS, 2014, p. 23).

From the very beginning of the arrival of Europeans on the African continent (when, for example, Nuno Tristao and his entourage entered the Geba River to capture slaves), African institutions were confronted with the problem of slavery (ACOSTA-LEYVA, 2016). However, "The reception of the indigenous people was not peaceful" (CAMMILLERI, 2010, p. 21), as Tristao and his entourage "were received with poisoned arrows [...]" (ACOSTA-LEYVA, 2016, p. 21). Consequently, all 22 men who were with Nuno Tristao died, including him, and those who didn't die were squires of Prince Henry the Navigator (ZURARA, 1948?, p. 222-223). This was how the advent of a visibly bloodthirsty era that would last for at least four centuries came about (CAMMILLERI, 2010, p. 21).

After the episode of Nuno Tristao, the Portuguese continued their explorations along the African coast, discovering lands in search of the way to the Indies in order to trade; however, they changed their tactics and strategies towards the natives in relation to obtaining slaves: "After this bitter experience, Lisbon changed its methods and instead of force, it began to use cunning exchange and trade." (CAMMILLERI, 2010, p. 21). "Since the arrival of the Portuguese caravels, probably in 1446, Portugal declared its mission to be that of bringing 'civilization' and salvation to the 'primitives' and Gentiles" (through evangelization) (MENDY, 1993, p. 5). Based on Peter Karibe Mendy's statements, it can be inferred that the Portuguese explorers began to spread the Catholic faith, although at the time they did so in a very insignificant way, with no relevant impact on present-day Guinea-Bissau: in this territory, which was partially Islamized, there were no Christian missions at the time. On the motives of the Portuguese at the time, Silva and Santos (2014, p. 23) write that

> Azurara, a sixteenth-century Portuguese historian who chronicled the region from 1450 onwards, in his "Cronica do Descobrimento e Conquista da Guine", mentions five reasons that would have motivated Prince Henry the Navigator to conquer Guinea:
> • The first reason had to do with wanting to get to know the lands beyond the Canary Islands and Cape Bojador;
> • The second reason was for commercial reasons, not to exchange products;
> • The third reason had to do with the need to ascertain whether the power of the Moors in that African land was much greater than had been reported;
> • The fourth reason was to find out if there would be any Christian kings in those parts, even if they had to make journeys into the interior of the territory;
> • The fifth reason was to expand the Christian faith.

The territory of present-day Guinea-Bissau was administered through Cape Verde (in Santiago) until 1879, when the territory became autonomous as a separate colony, with Bolama serving as its first capital. The Portuguese never penetrated the interior of their colonies, but only occupied the coast. This effectively shows that the autochthones resisted the Portuguese explorers.

Between 1884 and 1885, with the Berlin Conference organized by Bismark, the European powers ambitiously divided Africa without respecting local realities and without considering the interests of Africans in the process. Fourteen countries took part in the conference: the United Kingdom, the United States of America, France, Germany, the Austro-Hungarian Empire, the Ottoman Empire (now Turkey), Spain, Italy, Sweden, Russia, Denmark, Portugal, the Netherlands and Belgium. After this conference, the colonialists set about the actual occupation of African territories. In Africa, European colonialism lasted between 75 and 90 years, the latter period referring to Portuguese colonized territories, since, unlike France and England in the 1960s, Portugal refused decolonization. Colonialism in Africa took place much later than in the Americas, unlike in Brazil, for example, where it lasted for three centuries and twenty-two years.

In the past, it was the European traders who paid taxes to the native chiefs, as Augel said: "For a long period, from the 15th century to the middle of the 19th century, it was the Portuguese who paid tributes and other taxes to the local monarchs, including a residence tax" (2007, p. 56). After the effective occupation of the territory, the Portuguese began to collect taxes for their own purposes and to impose compulsory labor on the Africans. In 1895, "[...] it was decreed that all adult men had to pay a personal tax called 'imposto', as a sign of vassalage and above all as compensation for the military expenses faced by Portuguese troops during the pacification campaigns" (MENDY, 1993, apud CAMMILLERI, 2010, p. 22-23).

In the so-called Portuguese Guinea, "The period from 1913 to 1915 was marked by an upsurge in 'pacification', carried out with unusual violence by Commander Teixeira Pinto [...]." However, on the other hand, it should also be noted that, according to Henriques,

> The "pacification campaigns" carried out by Europeans to achieve the occupation of vast swathes of African territories resulted in decades of confrontation, repression and military efforts to impose a peace that would allow the installation of a system of exploitation of men and the valorization of colonies (2014, p. 50-51).

With this in mind, the Brasa people, "[...] who until then had tolerated the Portuguese presence with indifference, decided to provoke the war, claiming the pride of a free and independent people". To this end, "[...] they used cunning as a tactic: when the tax collectors arrived in a village, the adult men hid in the forest, leaving the women and children behind." (CAMMLLERI, 2010, p. 23). In short, it was the strategy they adopted to avoid paying taxes, as did the papiers and the bijagos. In fact, they were against paying the taxes imposed on them by the Portuguese. To this end, they waged an intense war against the Portuguese occupiers. It's important to note that the Papeis in particular refused to pay taxes, claiming that they owned the land (AUGEL, 2007, p. 56).

In 1940, the capital of the colony was moved from Bolama to Bissau. Before the administrative separation of Guinea-Bissau and Cape Verde, everything was done in Cape Verde, including the press and the printing press. This has to do with the neglect of what was then Portuguese Guinea, since it was of no economic interest at the time and, consequently, there was no white settlement. In Cape Verde, an uninhabited archipelago before the arrival of the first Portuguese, there was a process of creolization, understood as biological and cultural mixing between a few European settlers and African slaves. This process, which began as early as the 15th century, resulted in a reasonably homogeneous Creole people, unlike other territories of the then Senegambia, inhabited by several distinct ethnic groups. The Portuguese settlers and African slaves who populated the islands of Sao Tome and Principe from 1493 onwards were also undergoing a process of creolization. Let's take a look at what Gerhard Seibert said:

> The direct and prolonged encounter between Portuguese culture and the various African cultures in the two archipelagos generated a process of mutual acculturation: a Europeanization of the Africans, as well as an Africanization of the Europeans, which resulted in the emergence of two Creole societies with their own languages and cultures (2014, p. 44).

Consequently, in the 20th century, the Portuguese considered Cape Verdeans and Santomeans to be Creoles, Catholics, more "civilized", who were not subject to the status of indigenes. In 1926, the First Portuguese Republic implemented this discriminatory status in Angola and Mozambique and, subsequently, also in the then Portuguese Guinea, in 1927. The indigene status was applied only to the colonized of the three African territories on the continent, but not to the population of the two archipelagos or the populations of Goa, Macau and East Timor, as they were considered more "civilized".

This statute also laid down the conditions for an indigenous person to become assimilated and be formally equated with a Portuguese citizen: eat at the table, be Catholic, read and write Portuguese correctly, dress in the European style and behave well. In this context, it is worth emphasizing that compulsory labor was applied to the colonized. In 1961, the year the war of liberation began in Angola, which effectively shared a colonizer with Guinea-Bissau, international pressure grew and Adriano Moreira, the then Minister for Overseas Territories, abolished the Statute for Indigenous People.

During colonialism, at the end of the 19th century and the beginning of the 20th century, Africans were often seen by the colonialists as people without civilization or history and, moreover, they were branded as "backward" and "retarded" and, for this reason, they really needed to be civilized and converted to Christianity. It's also worth emphasizing that, in general, there were no Christian missions in Islamized regions. The colonizers really didn't take African realities into account, since Africans had a well-structured social and economic organization, different from the Portuguese reality. There were great civilizations in West Africa, such as Ghana, Mali and Kanem-Bornu. The colonialists, however, ignored African realities and their cultures, considering them inferior to European ones.

[a]After World War II, in the 1950s and 60s, the Portuguese tried to sustain and justify their ideology of permanence in order to maintain their dominance and exploit raw materials in African territories by mobilizing three main myths, highlighted by historian Isabel Castro Henriques:

> These three groups of myths, thought of in three dimensions - *anthropological* (the racial and cultural superiority of the white man and its corollary "the civilizing mission", *historical* (the founding role of the Portuguese discoveries in knowledge and the secular continuity of Portugal's presence in the world), *sociological* (the theory of lusotropicalism, Gilberto Freyre's theory of lusotropicalism, based on the uniqueness of the harmonious relationships always established by the Portuguese with other peoples, the virtues of "assimilation" and the evidence of the absence of national racism) - effectively and durably ensured the scientific justification and historical legitimacy of Portugal's colonial choices. (HENRIQUES, 2014, p. 6).

Due to the exploitation of man by man and Portuguese colonialism, the Party he African Union for the Independence of Guinea and Cape Verde (PAIGC) was created to end colonial rule on September 19, 1956, in Bissau, by Amilcar Lopes Cabral, Luis Cabral, Aristides Pereira, Julio de Almeida, Fernando Fortes and Elisde Turpin. From the beginning, it was chaired by Amilcar Lopes Cabral, the executive secretary. The PAIGC also had as its objective the unity of Guind and Cape Verde in order to free both from the Portuguese yoke, justifying that the

> [...] the story of Guind-Bissau's unity used to be defended on the basis of the centuries-old links between these two countries; links that go back to the "discovery" by Portuguese marines in 1460 of the apparently uninhabited archipelago (made up of ten islands), and its subsequent settlement with Portuguese adventurers, political exiles and criminals and African captives from the adjacent continent - especially from the regions of Cacheu and Bissau, the main Portuguese slave-trading centers. (MENDY, 1993, p. 26). [The historical links between Guind-Bissau and Cape Verde are truly irrefutable. These ties were strengthened during the national liberation struggle against the common colonizer, a bloody struggle carried out in the forests of Guind-Bissau in which Cape Verdeans made significant contributions (MENDY, 1993, p. 28).

In fact, the PAIGC tried to adhere to the ideology of socialism, but never explicitly adopted it. During the same period, Guinean workers also organized themselves:

> In 1958, the National Union of Guind Workers (UNTG) was created, also a clandestine trade union movement which, on August 3, 1959, provoked a general strike by dockers and sailors, workers at the port of Pindjiguiti, to protest against low wages, which was brutally repelled by the colonial forces (AUGEL, 2007, p. 61).

Around 50 dockers died in this massacre, a figure disputed by some scholars, who claim that there were only 9 deaths or even less. From then on, Cabral opted for the armed route in order to free himself from Portuguese domination. Furthermore, the PAIGC did everything it could to prevent an armed struggle and tried, unsuccessfully, to negotiate the independence of the two territories.

In 1960, the PAIGC moved to Guind-Conacry (an independent country since 1958) with the support of then-president Seku Tourd, who in fact welcomed it so that he could carry out his diplomatic policy and discuss guerrilla strategy in depth. The national liberation struggle began on January 23, 1963 in the Tite barracks, in the Quinara region, in the south of the country, with the first shot fired by Arafam Mane. The PAIGC fought against Portuguese colonialism for 11 years, until 1974. Earlier, in 1973, the party decided to declare Guind-Bissau's independence unilaterally, on September 24. Independence was proclaimed in Madina de Bod and Joao Bernardo Vieira, as the then President of the National Assembly, read his letter of declaration.

At the time, the unilateral declaration was recognized internationally by a resolution of the United Nations General Assembly by more than 80 countries. The process of independence was different from that of the other territories of the then Portuguese colonial empire, since they all gained their independence in 1975, after the fall of the Portuguese dictatorship by the Revolution of April 25, 1974. At the time of independence, Luis Cabral, Amilcar Cabral's half-brother, became President of the Republic of Guind-Bissau and Francisco Mendes, alias Tchico-Td, became Prime Minister. After negotiations with the PAIGC, Portugal recognized

Guind-Bissau's independence on 10 September 1974.

Even before the declaration of independence, on January 20, 1973, Amilcar Lopes Cabral was assassinated in Conacry. To date, no one can say for sure who the main mastermind of the crime was. However, the following have been accused of being complicit in Cabral's death: Sekou Tourd, former president of Guind-Conacry, Nino Vieira and his cousin Osvaldo Vieira; however, their involvement in the assassination of the PAIGC's charismatic leader has not been established.

After the country's emancipation, it became clear that there were too few trained staff to be able to carry out sustainable and consolidated development. "[...] the number of Guineans with an academic degree was no more than fourteen, to which were added only seventeen with a medium degree, which shows the deplorable state of Portugal's lack of interest in this colony." (AUGEL, 2007, p. 73). In fact, Portugal had not only shown a lack of interest in its former colonies, but also in its territory with regard to higher education, since it was only in 1910, with the advent of the First Republic, that other universities were opened, apart from the University of Coimbra, founded in the 13th century. Until then, this university was the only one that functioned.

Seven years after independence, in 1980, there was a military coup that overthrew the first President of Guind-Bissau, who had not been democratically elected but had been chosen by the PAIGC to preside over the new country. The military coup, led by Joao Bernardo Vieira alias Nino Vieira, was justified by the coup plotters as being a "Readjustment Movement", claiming that they carried out the coup in light of the numerous executions of people that had taken place under the government of Lrns Cabral. In addition, the coup plotters claimed that there was a deep economic crisis in the country and, after the coup, Nino Vieira took over the presidency of the Republic. As a result, it can be considered that in the first period after independence,

> Both during Luis Cabral's time and in the period that followed, practically until the beginning of the 1990s, the *status quo* was imposed through force and arrogance, the secret service, imprisonment, the elimination of opponents and the repression of all resistance. Corruption, nepotism and cronyism dominated (AUGEL, 2007, p. 64).

In 1986, there was the so-called "October 17 affair", in which those accused of orchestrating a coup to overthrow Nino were barbarously shot. Those executed were mostly Brasa people, as among those shot we have the following names: Paulo Correia, 1st Vice-President of the Council of State of Guinea-Bissau and Minister of Justice and Local Power and Dr. Viriato Pa, the then Attorney General of the Republic, among other innocent people, executed despite international protests, namely: "[...] the Pope himself and the Portuguese President, Mario Soares." (SILVA; SANTOS, 2014, p. 271).

In the context of democratization in Africa in 1991, Nino Vieira's regime also ushered in multipartyism and political openness, in other words, Guinea-Bissau experienced democratic rule in its constitution. Three years later, the first multi-party elections were held, in which Nino Vieira won in the second round, defeating Kumba Yala of the newly-created Social Renewal Party (PRS). As a result, Nino Vieira was the first democratically elected president in the Republic of Guinea-Bissau.

In 1998, Brigadier Ansumane Mane was "accused (by Nino) of incuria in the trafficking of arms to the independentists of Casamanga (Senegal)." (CARDOSO, 2000, p. 87). This attitude led Nino to dismiss Mane and appoint a new brigadier, Humberto Gomes. Furthermore, "The accusations of arms trafficking were just the straw that broke the camel's back." (CARDOSO, 2000, p. 89-90). On the one hand, and on the other, Mane's resignation conditioned the military uprising.

Nino, for his part, without the consent of the People's National Assembly, decided to bring in military personnel from Senegal and Guinea-Conakry to support him, sparking the civil war, which began on June 7, 1998. On the basis of these statements, Professor Fode Mane puts it this way:

> we have not found the source of legitimacy for the actions of foreign soldiers in the conflict." Furthermore, "If recourse to rape by the military itself in order to resolve an internal situation is illegitimate, the response adopted by the authorities was not the one permitted by domestic law either. (MANE, 2000, p. 76).

During this civil war, a lot of damage was done to the capital, including the destruction of the National Institute of Studies and Research (INEP). This research institution was actually turned into a barracks for the foreign military, instead of being protected, as was done with the banks (KOUDAWO, 2000, p. 9). What's more, INEP's archives were in fact burned, as foreign troops used them to set fires. However, despite suffering from the military conflict, INEP was "also one of the institutions that was able to recover most quickly from the disaster caused by the conflict" (KOUDAWO, 2000, p. 5).

Finally, in May 1999, this 11-month military conflict came to an end, with the defeat and exile of Nino Vieira in Portugal. After Nino's departure, a government of National Unity was formed, with Malam Bacai Sanha as interim President and Francisco Josd Fadul as interim Prime Minister. In the same year, presidential and legislative elections were held. The PRS and the RGB (Resistance of Guinea Bissau), also known as the Bafata Movement, won the legislative elections. Kumba Yala, president of the PRS, was elected President of the Republic.

The accusation of Yala's arbitrary use of power and the deep economic crises the country was facing led the military, especially in the person of Verissimo Seabra, to overthrow Yala in a military coup on September 14, 2003. As a result, they formed a government of National Unity in which religious organizations and civil society participated. These organizations chose Henrique Pereira Rosa as interim President and Artur Sanha as interim Prime Minister.

In 2004, legislative elections were held in which the PAIGC won, electing Carlos Gomes Junior, its President, to serve as Prime Minister. The following year, with the return of then General Nino Vieira to the country after six years in exile in Portugal, presidential elections were also held. Nino Vieira, as an independent candidate, won this ballot for the post of Head of State in the second round, defeating Malam Bacai Sanha, the PAIGC candidate. Unfortunately, on April 1, 2009, there was a bomb attack on the Armed Forces Headquarters, in which General Tagme Na Waie died. The following day, in retaliation, Nino Vieira was shot dead by the military at his home. The President of the People's National Assembly, Raimundo Pereira, then took over as interim president. Jose Zamora Induta took over on an interim basis as Chief of the General Staff of the Armed Forces (CEMGFA), and has remained in office. So far, rumors of a drug trafficking relationship behind these crimes have not been proven.

On April 12, 2012, on the eve of the campaign for the 2nd[a] round of the presidential election, the military once again staged a coup d'état, led by Antonio Injai, in which the then Prime Minister Carlos Gomes Junior was deposed. It was alleged that there had been a secret military agreement between the government of Guinea-Bissau and that of Angola, in which the military had petitioned the Angolan Military Mission (MISSANG) to hand over the equipment they had brought from Angola in order to support Guinea-Bissau. This military coup was repudiated by the international community, particularly the European Union and the CPLP. Consequently, the military leaders were sanctioned by the international community.

With the mediation of the Community of West African States (ECOWAS), especially Nigeria, a transitional government was formed, which lasted two years and ended up frustrating the expectations of the Guinean people, who were so suffering and optimistic about better days to come. Despite the many things that have happened in their eyes, the Guinean people have been indifferent, demanding nothing, even if their rights are being violated. What's more, for some Guineans, the only people to blame for the country's political instability are the "Balanta" military, who are branded as coup plotters, rebels and troublemakers.

In 2014, Guinea-Bissau once again held legislative and presidential elections. The

PAIGC won both elections, with Domingos Simoes Pereira, President of the PAIGC, elected Prime Minister and Jose Mario Vaz (JOMAV) as Head of State. The elections were successful and the Guinean population was once again optimistic about the new government, despite the many political uncertainties the country was experiencing. In this context, it was thought that this government would lead the country out of chaos and deadlock and towards the development desired by the Guinean people. However, on August 12, 2015, JOMAV dismissed the government of Domingos Simoes Pereira, despite appeals from many national and international organizations. The former United Nations Special Representative in Guinea-Bissau, the Timorese Jose Ramos-Horta, also pleaded against the dismissal. Despite his pleas, JOMAV dismissed the government on the grounds that there were irregularities, nepotism and widespread corruption on the part of the members of Domingos Simoes Pereira's government.

The rift and political imbroglio between the Domingos Simoes Pereira wing and the JOMAV wing in the PAIGC, in turn, had a strong impact on Guinean society and the people, fortunately, finally protested against the act before the government was deposed. Even so, their demands were not heard by JOMAV, who saw fit to dismiss the government in order to combat the aforementioned issues. Despite this, the Brasa military, considered to be "coup-plotters", did not speak out about the government figures dismissed by JOMAV, namely Domingos Simoes Pereira and Carlos Correia, the latter of whom had only been in office for almost eight months. Even so, the climate of instability continues to this day.

Regarding political instability in Guinea-Bissau, Couto and Embalo (2010, 26-27) stated that "a superficial observer could come to the conclusion that the country is ungovernable, that Guineans (and Africans in general) cannot live in a democracy and, finally, that they are not prepared to live in today's capitalist and globalized world." However, "this is a fallacious conclusion."

2.1 IDENTITY OF THE BRASA PEOPLE

The Brasa[3] are a majority ethnic group in Guinea-Bissau, spread across different territories of the country. The name Balanta came about when they refused to submit to the yoke of the Mandinka people; in Mandinka the term is *abalanta* which means: those who do not submit; those who refuse to be subjugated; rebels. Carreira (1959) apud Cammileri also

[3] This term has been spelled Brassa and/or Braza by other authors: however, I have decided to write the commonly used spelling. Other common terms appear throughout this work and have been written in brackets to make the content easier to understand. In addition, it should be noted that according to the convention established by the Brazilian Anthropology Association in 1953, the names of indigenous people, on the one hand, should be spelled with a capital letter and, on the other, should not be written in plural (FIORIN; PETTER, 2014).

made the following assertions:

> [...] the term 'Balanta' in the Mandingo language is expressed as: *ebalanta.* Breaking down this word you get: E (they), - *bala* (deny), - *nta* (repetitive morpheme) = they keep denying, refusing, rebelling; thus the rebels, the indomitable and the refractory [...] the very ones "are called Brasa." (CAMMILLERI, 2010, p. 15)

And even today they are sometimes labeled that way, pejoratively. But they themselves "[...] define themselves as those who remain uninterrupted, the valid, the authentic, the strong" (CAMMILLERI, 2010, 17).

2.2 SOCIO-POLITICAL ORGANIZATION OF THE BRASA

The Brasa people have a gerontocratic society, whose organization is similar to that of the Beafada and the Nalu, while at the same time it is different from the organization of the majority of the peoples of GuiC-Bissau. Thus, "The Balanta, Beafada and Nalu are aedapal ethnic groups, while the Fula and Mandinka have a more defined hierarchical structure. The Balanta are animists, while the Fula, Mandinga, Beafada and Nalu are, to varying degrees, Islamized." (OLIVEIRA, 1996, p. 25). More specifically, the Brasa have a horizontal political structure, i.e. they are "stateless" and have two Community Bodies, namely: the Council of Ancestors, made up exclusively of circumcised men *(bilante bindag),* and the Council of Ancestors, made up only of married women. It is worth quoting Cammilleri (2010, p. 87), who emphasizes: "[...] the Brasa have created a system of power that is not centralized in one person of a lineage, but is shared by all the heads of extended families who guarantee unity and collaboration."

The Council of Ancies discusses exclusively the many problems that concern them and holds its meetings to defend women's interests. For example, if a woman from the *tabanka* (village) were to commit some nefarious practice, such as adultery. The Council of Ancestors will be in charge of dealing with this matter, and big men cannot interfere in it, even if it's the wife of an elder responsible for the *fram*[4] . On the other hand, as far as the Council of Elders is concerned, their duties are far greater, since they discuss various problems that concern men and the *tabanka*, such as: the performance of the fanado (initiation ritual), the fate of the *tabanka*, encouraging young people to perform any cultural manifestation that hasn't been performed for a long time, punishing offenders, among other competencies.

Generally speaking, these bodies are made up of capable people who jointly make decisions regarding the well-being of the *tabanka* and serve to resolve any problems it may

[4] This *fram* is usually in the middle of the *moransa* where an elder is chosen regardless of his social status; if he has a good conduct, the *moransa* chooses him to be an intermediary between *Ira* (God) and the *moransa*.

have. No one within the *tabanka* dares to violate the decisions of these bodies, because if they do, they will certainly be punished in accordance with the rules established by them.

The Brasa are divided into two main subgroups: those from *Kuntoi* and those from *Nhacra,* the latter known as *Buungue* or outsiders (RITH, 2013, p. 1)5. The Brasa from Nhacra migrate more than those from *Kuntoi.* Therefore,

> On the left bank of the Mansoa River (from source to mouth) are the Balantas of Nagra (or Nhacra). They are also called Buwungue (meaning Birds)" [...] since the Balanta Nhacra migrate more. "Perhaps this is the name by which they are called in the Balanta language and culture: Buwungue (migratory birds). (RITH, 2013, p. 1).

In addition, the Balanta of Nhakra migrate to different zones, especially the next zone, due to their many activities:

> Their migratory destination [the Balanta (Brasa) Nhacra] is both to the west and to the north and south of the country. Towards the west, they move to regions such as Biombo and Quinhamel, where they form their settlements in the territory of the Papel ethnic group (in Balanta, Beza-o, hence the origin of the name of the capital city of the Republic of Guinea-Bissau, which is the result of the spelling of its name in the Balanta language). In reference to the Mansoa River (which runs through Guinea-Bissau from the center to the west), the Balantas of Kuntowe are located on the right bank of the river (from the source to the mouth, i.e. from the interior to the sea). Another destination for Buwungue emigration is traditionally to the south of Guinea, crossing the Geba River by canoe (RITH, 2013, p. 1).

On the other hand, the Brasa of Kuntoi migrate infrequently. They, in turn, "migrate north towards Ingore and Farim, where they cross paths with the Mandinka people, converting to the Muslim religion as a result of the influence of local traditions" (RITH, 2013, p. 1). It is worth emphasizing that the Brasa people mix with the other peoples of Guinean territory through nuptials, especially with the Pepel and the Mandinga (RITH, 2013, p. 1). In fact, this mixing occurs more on the part of Brasa women.

The Brasa have a patrilineal lineage, although both the maternal uncle and the maternal aunt have many privileges and attributions regarding their nephews and nieces; the latter have the right to educate them from the age of five until adulthood and, if it's a girl, the maternal aunt is the one who will educate her and offer her in marriage to anyone in the *moransa* (a group of houses in a patrilineal clan), even to her husband if he has any interest in her. As far as the boy is concerned, it is the maternal uncle who decides when he should become a *land dag,* in other words, it is the maternal uncle who takes the lead in deciding whether or not to go to the *fanado, in* order to become a grown man so that he can take part in the Community Organ. [5]

[5] Available at: <http://tchogue.blogspot.com.br/2013/06/frehu-n-flif-n-13-composicao-da-familia.html>

ТашЬёш, the maternal uncle is the only person who can take you away from your father's house if you are seriously ill. When going to the fanado, paternal uncles are not allowed to touch their nephews and the maternal uncle must be vigilant on that day so that nothing bad happens to his nephew, since on that day the mathematical people take the opportunity to do something bad to the candidates for the fanado. Because of the importance of the maternal uncle in both the social and spiritual life of his nephews, parents warn their children to respect and love their uncles.

2.3 FAMILY COMPOSING IN THE HEART OF THE COALS

The composition of the Brasa family is as follows: the sons stay in the *moransa* and marry and have the right to belong to that family, while the daughters, in view of the nuptials, do not stay in their father's house and so their children do not have the right to use the family name[6] (RITH, 2013, p. 1). Next, with regard to their administrative organization, in a *tabanka*, which concentrates the large family; the sons have the right to build their houses next to their father's, that is, around their father's house, with the aim of leaving a large space within the community, where they build *fram*. (RITH, 2013, p. 1).

2.4 BRASA PEOPLE'S AGE GROUPS

> Among the Balantas, the individual does not exist in an isolated and abstract singularity, but in his participation in different groups: kinship and alliance, age, locality and neighborhood. His status derives from the various functions he assumes, i.e. the set of reciprocal rights and duties that correspond to the various positions he occupies (IMBALI, 1992, p. 15-16).

The age group among the Brasa follows the stages of formation according to the distribution of tasks from the moment a particular person from the same group is able to perform any function for the *tabanka*, particularly the *moransa*. Most of the work they do is done in groups because, for the Brasa, working in groups strengthens the bonds of friendship and social cohesion. As a result, from an early age they learn to value others through teamwork.

2.5 STAGES IN THE FORMATION OF MEN

Accessed: June 26, 2015.

[6] Available at: <http://tchogue.blogspot.com.br/2013/06/frehu-n-flif-n-13-composicao-da-familia.html> Access: June 26, 2015.

With regard to the stages of formation of the Brasa, especially the men, it should be stressed that the same society "[...] has continued to retain its identity to this day thanks to its social organization based on the division of age groups for each of the two sexes". (CAMMILLERI, 2010, p. 79). These stages will be described below.

2.5.1 Bidokn Ni Nhari: first stage of training for men

It's a group made up of boys aged 6 to 12, and from then on the life of a Brasa begins. A boy at this age herds cattle. The boys of a particular *tabanka* lead the cattle to a suitable place to graze. Sometimes the journey from home to this place is up to five kilometers. When they reach their destination, they leave the cattle there in a group, and all those present keep watch so as not to lose sight of any animal. There are always the big boys, who keep order by coordinating the others.

It's at this stage that they begin to learn how to fight and unite. The older ones always tell the younger ones off, if an animal is going too far, to make it come back and join the others.

Then there are the following stages of formation: *nthokfos,* which starts between the ages of 13 and 15 and literally means lighting a match. They are effectively errand boys for the elders, with the task of buying oil and phosphors so that the house can be lit at night; they also have the job of buying tobacco for the elders and are trusted adolescents, as they are the ones who carry secret messages. During rice cultivation, they bring water to the rice farmers, as this is when the work of rice farming begins. To do this, the father of each member of this group builds a plow for them, so that they begin to know how to use it to cultivate the land (CAMMILLERI, 2010, p. 62-63).

Next, *n'gwac [n'guatch*] is the stage that begins between the ages of 16 and 17, and is the training of young people who are skilled at doing any task in the *tabankas*, especially working in the rice fields. For this reason, "[...] they are skilled boatmen, capable of pushing and maneuvering long canoes tens of meters long, loaded with rice, straw and cattle" (CAMMILLERI, 2010, p. 63).

The training stage for *n 'kuman* lasts from 18 to 21 years; this group's function is to learn how to cut down different trees (CAMMILLERI, 2010, p. 64), to maintain order at any *tabanka* event and to carry out the work skillfully; therefore, "The group's emblem is the turtle *(nkubur), an* animal that is the symbol of physical endurance and wisdom." (CAMMILLERI, 2010, p. 64). (CAMMILLERI, 2010, p. 64). Furthermore, according to Cammilleri (2010, p. 64), the n'kumans "represent the main force of farming in the rice paddies; to this end, they set challenges and organize real competitions of work speed between all the farmers or between the groups where each one makes their strength and skill count."

The group of *n'ghaies* is made up of young people aged between 22 and 25. This is the most entertaining phase in the *tabanka.* During this phase they go barefoot and shirtless even if they are going to a distant place; their symbols are the cow's horn and the ram's horn to extract sounds; They grease their whole body with white mud, build a palm straw bag to put their food in every *moransa* they arrive at, among other habits; the lamas that the *N'Ghaies* wear are the uniforms that identify them as such; they also wear *malila, lope,* chains and their role in the *tabanka* is to fight.

Then they enter another phase, called *n'ghes.* This is when sexual life begins, because on the day of entering the *n'ghes* phase, the *blufu bindag* (big young men) first talk to the *binan'ghas* (girls aged 18 to 20 who come from other *tabankas* to date) about having a relationship with the *n'ghes*. These girls always accept the courtship, because they are guided by the big women for this important moment for both them and the *N'ghaies.*

Then, the *n'ghaies* are usually surprised one night to perform this symbolic ceremony, i.e. the *blufu bindag* take the *n'ghaies* by force to have sexual relations with these *binan'ghas.* From that moment on, the *n'ghaies* are free to start their love life in order to get married. In this ceremony, the *n'ghaies* are usually taken to the house where those *binan'ghas* were received, and they spend a week receiving advice from the *blufu bindag* in order to behave well with their girlfriends and also with their future wives, giving them the respect they deserve as a way of honoring the name of their family and the *moransa.*

Figure 2 - Group of *N'ghaies*

Source: IBD (April 22, 2014)[7]

Figure 3 - Group of *N'ghes*

Source: IBD (Apr. 22, 2014) .[8]

The *blufu bindag* stage begins between the ages of 26 and 30. It's a stage of preparation for adulthood, because it's where a lufu dag prepares to be a grown man; however, in order to be a grown man, he has to be *fanned*, i.e. leave his youth behind and take on the responsibility of being the "head" of his family. At this stage, even if a *lufu dag* has a wife, he doesn't yet have the skills to run his own family, and the one who does is a *lad dag.*

The *lad dag* stage is the last, and means that he is an educated person who is qualified to be part of the Council of Elders. After the occasion of the *fanaticism,* a *land dag* is called a new *lambe*, as Cammilleri postulates,

> The new *lambe* are easily recognizable because they wear a red wool hat on their head with the tip of the brim falling forward over their forehead. Only at the end of the successive *fo* ritual, which takes place in the area, will the brim of the hat be turned to the side and fall over the right ear. It is on this occasion that the *lambe* take on a new name and the title of ALANTE NDAN (adult, responsible and elderly man). (CAMMILLERI, 2010, p. 86).

Therefore, he is a *fanado* and is respected in any *tabankas* of the Brasa; he wears a red cap called by the Brasa *fibague faf*

2.6 STAGES OF WOMEN'S EDUCATION

Among the Brasa, unlike men, women do not go through the initiation rite. For women to reach puberty, there is a whole formative process which is divided into a number of phases, just as it is for men. These phases will be described in the next few lines:

2.6.1 Nbifula Sonh (Girl)

This age group is made up of girls from 0 to 10 years old; it is a preparatory phase for girls, in which they are taught domestic activities for adolescent life.

The next stage, *nbifula ndan* (adolescent), is entered between the ages of 11 and 15; these are young teenagers who, in effect, are being prepared to discern what is good and bad in order to face marriage and take on responsibilities from now on, especially taking care of a family and instructing the girls and boys who will grow up there.

The *iegle* stage (bride in the Brasa language) takes place between the ages of 16 and 18. The *legleë* is a newlywed bride and, stripped of her old personalities, she will begin to fulfill the duties of a wife from that moment on, respecting both her husband and the women of the following stages, with whom she dare not argue, even if she is right. Finally, the bride, "To reach her full maturity, all she needs is the guidance of the master so *that she* can move on to the next stage *(thata) [fata]*[7] ." (CAMMILLERI, 2010, p. 51).

When a woman in the following stages of her life frustrates her expectations and hurts her sensibilities, she should seek the advice of the ancients to resolve her problem, and the same applies if the complaint is against her husband; they will analyze the case and attribute the blame to the person who hurt her and the person will be fined according to the decisions of the council of ancients. She cannot do anything without first consulting these women, because it is they who will help her to mature and become a visionary with regard to solving any problems and carrying out the *tabanka*'s tasks.

It should be noted that if an iegle's husband dies, after all the funeral ceremonies she has the right to choose who she would like to marry in the same *tabanka*; the person who remarries her will take care of her.

After *iegle* we have the following stages: *fata, sade, anin ndolo*, which are not defined by a specific age, but rather by experiences accumulated over the years, which will give these women of different stages the attributes and skills to make the big decisions of both punishing a woman when she has committed adultery and supporting her in getting married. In addition, the *Fata* phase includes

> After the birth of the second child, the *iegle* is called *thata [fata]*, but this period ends when the woman expresses the desire to go on a long journey, [...] The reasons are diverse: visits to distant relatives, seasonal work activities, pilgrimages to the

[7] My emphasis.

> sanctuary of the family's original territory and others. No one can oppose this right, not even the husband. In fact, it is a sign of her independence and a right recognized by tradition. When she returns, she begins to fulfill her duties (CAMMILLERI, 2010, p. 51). [With the end of the fertile period and the beginning of the menopause, the brazilian woman is recognized as *Sade*, which is the phase of introduction into the activity of command. [She] is recognized as very important to the family community [...] and feared for the danger that can come from menstrual blood. (CAMMILLERI, 2010, p. 52).

It is also his job to look after women when they give birth and to go to the fortune-teller if a woman falls ill in the *tabanka.* Finally, the last stage *is* the *anin n 'dolo* phase. The women of this stage are feared by people in the *tabanka*, everyone respects them for their age and their life experience, even if it's a *lad dag*, they don't dare offend her under any circumstances, she *is* always consulted when making any decision in the *tabanka.*

> A word from you *[anin n'dolo],* a piece of advice from you, your approval or disapproval have a great influence on the thinking and behavior of others.

> young people and adults. It is especially consulted in solving serious problems in marital, family and village life (CAMMILLERI, 2014, p. 55).

2.7 BRASA ECONOMY: RICE CULTIVATION

The economy of the Brasa is based mainly on rice production, which is also crucial to the social relations of this ethnic group. According to OLIVEIRA et al. (1996, p. 368) "The Balanta, the largest ёйкс group in GuiC-Bissau, are the main cultivators of rice ("malu" in Balanta)." Before the Brasa start growing rice, the elder in charge of a clan goes to the *fram* where he makes the petition, ceremony and prayer for an abundance of rice. Only after this ceremony at the *fram* do they start growing rice. They do this because the Brasa believe that *Ira* can make sure that there is plenty of rice in the field.

The Brasa are also "recognized experts in the field, since colonial times they have often worked on land conquered from the sea by means of dams." (HANDEM, 1986, p. 56). The Brasa were interested in the south of the country, especially the area belonging to the Nalu people, as it was a suitable place for growing rice (RITH, 2013, p. 1). This has led many of them to migrate to the above-mentioned places in order to grow rice for their survival.

On the one hand, and on the other, rice cultivation "is a work process that is alternately male and female. It involves simple intra-family cooperation. The men plow the field around the house, uproot and bury the weeds, and the women sow the rice by pressing it into the ground." (HANDEM, 1986, p. 60). The Brasa do this activity in the rice field with great pleasure and everyone in the *moransa* participates without exception in order to show an action of solidarity between *moransas.* If there are few of them in the *moransa,* they hire some friends from another *tabanka* to help them in this arduous endeavor. In addition,

> The main exchange value of the *Arassa* economy [Brasa] and increasingly present in religious rituals, rice plays an essential role in social relations. The performance of socio-religious rituals that are transcendent for *Arassa* society, as well as all socio-political acts, are a function of the volume of the rice harvest [...] because rice is the main element in Arassa commercial contacts (HANDEM, 1986, p. 65).

Every day they make food for the rice farmers and, when they have finished, they sacrifice a few pigs to give to their helpers as a token of payment; they don't see this as a form of payment, but rather as a simple act of brotherhood and communion and some of them, in turn, do *Broska* (Brasa style dancing). Of course, rice "In order to constitute the basic element of their diet, *maale* interferes in all their socio-cultural manifestations." (HANDEM, 1986, p. 64).

3 KUSSUNDE AND ITS DYNAMICS

Even today, dance plays a very important role in society, including the *Kussunde* dance, which continues to have a great impact on the Brasa people. *Kussundeë* is a dance-party that takes place through competition between different groups of young people and teenagers who make up a particular *tabanka*, or even between different *tabankas*.

Kussunde is used to celebrate the rice harvest festival through euphoria and entertainment, to make the *tabanka* visible and to dazzle the other *tabankas*. It is usually held when there is an abundance of food. What's more, the fruits of the Brasa's various crops, specifically rice, "are used to cover the costs of the *ksunde (Kussunde)* [...]" (CAMMILLERI, 2010, p. 66). The Brasa perform this dance to show a year of prosperity and abundance, giving thanks and showing appreciation and recognition, paying tribute to their ancestors and their Iras for their clemency and protection of the *tabanka*. *Kussundeë* is one of the most decisive dangas among the Brasa, because it is associated with supernatural spirits and each group seeks out a diviner in order to make pacts to overcome it. Obviously,

> this danga was created by our ancestors from the first balanta in the world to the present day, in other words, this danga was created to share ideas and friendships between villagers, mainly to showcase the talents of the new generations[10] . *[Kussunde]*[11] is organized and developed
> usually under the responsibility of the head of the *blufu ndan (blufu bindag)* (CAMMILLERI, 2010, p. 66).

Furthermore, the *blufu bindag,* in Brasa language, define the rules to be followed between different groups. Each group in the danga has a leader who represents it and it is up to the leaders of the *blufu bindag* to arrange a meeting of the constituent groups. The heads of the constituent groups encourage their members to raise money in order to go to a *balobeiro, i*.e. a fortune-teller.

In addition, *the blufu bindag, n'ghaies*, and above all *n'kuman* are responsible for structuring the place where the guests stay and maintaining order so that everything is impeccable, in order to please the spectators. It is customary for the big youngsters to go to their opponent's *tabanka* to request the *Kussunde* dance. When they go to that *tabanka*, they take cana bordao, or brandy, and tobacco, in order to ask the members of that *tabanka* to take part in the *Kussunde* contest to celebrate the abundance in the *tabankas*. The request for the *kussunde* is usually made in November and December, or rather, at the end of the harvest. When there is a good harvest in almost all the *tabankas* in Guinea-Bissau, particularly in the

---

[10] Interview given by Fambe via video call, Oct. 2015. It is important to note that the names given to the interviewees are fictitious.
[11] My emphasis.

tabankas where a significant number of the Brasa live, *kussunde* can sometimes take place even if there is not an abundance of food in the *tabankas*.

The date of the *Kussunde* is usually between April, May and June. When the *blufu binddg* arrive at the *tabanka* where they have gone to request the *Kussunde*, they ask the elders if they can receive them. If so, they define how the proposal will be made and what the criteria will be. The envoys take answers back to their *tabanka* in order to inform their partners how they were received by their opponents. They then meet with the people in their *tabanka*, who may confirm that the *Kussunde* dance will take place. If they do, they send the *blufu binddg* to inform the people in the *tabanka* where they went to make the request that the *Kussunde* dance has been confirmed. From then on, it is the responsibility of the elders to make arrangements to start the ceremony in all the sacred places of the *tabanka*, in order to negotiate with *Irds*. In this negotiation, they establish what the method will be, i.e. the means of payment to defeat the opponents. In fact, according to popular belief, the payment for the pact established can be the physical death of a person or the death of animals, depending on the pact they have made with the *Irds*[12] All the inhabitants of the *tabanka* take part in the *Kussunde*, since when a *tabanka* wins, it is a source of pride for everyone.

The anciaos and ancias don't participate directly in the danga because of their old age and their responsibilities with other *tabanka* tasks. However, they contribute in different ways to show their solidarity and sympathy for the dangarinos. In view of their contributions, the dangarinos feel confident and hold their heads high to win the competition, because there is a lot of rivalry and, above all, the prestige of the *tabanka* is at stake.

There are two types of *Kussunde:* one that takes place in the same *tabanka* and another that is danced in another *tabanka*. However, the most competitive is the one that is danced between *tabankas;* in it, each *tabanka* shows its bravery, its power and its ability. The dangarinos rehearse the *Kussunde* dance for a month inside the *moransa*, at night, because of their activities during the day.

The organizing committee (in this case, the *blufu bindag* group*)* places two or more containers on the dance site, far apart from each other; naturally, the dangarinos move away from the *moransas* in order to dangle in a secluded place. At the time of the dance, the spectators keep their eyes on the groups that are dancing and each one chooses which of the groups they want to support. A maximum of four *n'ghaies* can dangle on top of the container. When one group of *n'ghaies* finishes, another goes up to dangle, and so on until the end. Some of the spectators film the dance.

---

[12] Interview given by Sofis Namara in July 2015 via video call.

There are people at the time of the dance who occasionally put the protagonists who are singing on their shoulders to boast and exalt themselves in order to cause fear in their rivals and not give them any room to maneuver. Some spectators sometimes go up to the stage to offer money to a dangarino because he has danced well; others don't even go up, but go near the container where they are dangling and offer it. When a dangarino receives some gifts, he gives them to a trusted person to keep. Also at *Kussunde* "[...] the spectators encourage the dangarinos with shouts, exclamations of admiration, and show their enthusiasm by putting money notes in their own clothes [...]." (ZEMP, 2013, p. 46) when they are dangling well, which has a stimulating effect, which is why the dangarinos show off more in front of the spectators and try to contribute more to giving their best. By dangling well, they impress the audience even more and they shout, whistle and boo even more out of euphoria as a way of expressing their joy, emotion and support.

In this dance, too, "no matter what the individual in the inner world of a dangarino may be like, feelings are culturally codified, as soon as they are put into action as dance." (YOUNGERMAN, 2013, p. 81). This, in effect, makes dangarinos more appreciated, attractive and recognized for their myths and their qualities in enchanting spectators. The dangarinos induce the people of the *tabanka* to boast about their merit and their achievements through dance. This merit attracts the attention of many people, especially the girls, who become interested in getting married in the *tabanka*, because it represents prestige and prestige for them.

3.1 KUSSUNDE DANCE GROUPS

This dance is made up of three groups: *nghaies, dany kussunde* and *n'guatch,* commonly known as *m'pebe.* Furthermore, "The basis for organizing the groups is age, but only boys who have not yet undergone the fanado [initiation rite] can take part." (KIPP, 2005, p. 1)[13] . Women who are actually part of the *dany kussunde* group also take part, as mentioned above. The *dany kussunde group,* which performs entertainment for the *n'ghaies* who are competing, wears a uniform called *nbasam tindjidu.* They also wear a scarf, which the girls tie behind their heads. They also wear a comb cloth and mirrors adorned on it. These mirrors represent brilliance and are used to attract people. The function of this group is to sing and beat small boards to animate the dance. *Dany kussunde* uses jewelry to make bazofia, something that wasn't used much in ancient times.

The *n'ghaies* wear bijago skirts, *duck* (mango coconut), *bus* (buzio) and panopasan.

[13] Available at: <http://senegambia.blogspot.com.br/2005/08/guin-bissau-aspectos-da-vida-de-um_19.html>. Accessed on: August 7, 2015.

The *n'ghaies* also wear *lope, kata* and helmets. They also wear sheep's headdress, *n'faia, a* traditional skirt made from *blafe* bark and *yotch* (malila). The *m'pebeë* group is made up of boys and girls. The boys wear lengo on their heads to dangle *Kussunde* and dress like the "women", because they comb their hair, wear a blouse, earrings, and a tied lengo on their heads, locally known as *mara bu sobra*. They also use gazelle horns and monkey tails in the danga act as adornment, to show off. The girls in the group wear the same costumes as the boys.

When the day of the *Kussunde* arrives, the *blufu bindag* of the *tabanka* who have asked for the event to take place have to perform a dance action called *gronka*, in Brasa language, to confirm the route of the *tabankas* who are going to take part in the *Kussunde*. The day before the *gronka*, i.e. a training session for the dance, the *N'ghaies* prepare for the clash and usually do this *gronka* before they have moved to their opponents' *tabanka*.

In fact, the spectators and dangarinos from the other *tabankas* make their way for six to eight hours, depending on the distance from their opponents' *tabanka*; when they arrive at their destination, the Amphritrians arrange for the spectators to be received, especially the *N'Ghaies*, and they, in turn, are always the second group, after the spectators, to arrive at the site. They get up from their *tabankas* at a time that will allow them to arrive in the evening. In fact, most people come from different *tabankas* to watch the *Kussunde* and are from different age groups who evidently take part in this dance-party. Thus, it can be emphasized that, "The *ksunde (Kussunde)* is expected and participated in by everyone [...]" (CAMMILLERI, 2010, p. 66).

The spectators of the challenging *tabanka* move around in order to find the hosts, taking shortcuts so that the opponents don't see them, while the receivers are usually on the lookout for the challengers so as not to step on the places they consider strategic. In these places, the opponents can negotiate with their rivals' *Iras* to win the dance, giving them what they asked for. On the way to the *tabanka* where they will perform the *Kussunde* dance, they often fight over the violation of spaces forbidden by receivers, or rather, by the owners of the *tabanka* where the *Kussunde* dance takes place, because these places are considered essential to winning the *Kussunde*, as their secrets are buried there. They are also places where the *N'Ghaies* can effectively negotiate *Kussunde*'s victory[14] . In spite of everything, when they see each other, they rejoice and go to be guided by receivers as to how they should walk to enter the host *tabanka*, and set off for the place of the dance .[15]

When the contingents arrive, the *N'Ghaies* are forced to sleep in one place to prevent information from leaking out about their arrival, so that people don't know where they've been.

[14] Interview given by Bihinha Namara, in Aug. 2015, on Facebook.
[15] Interviews with different people during my stay at GuiiL-Bissaii.

If an enemy knows, they can inform their adversaries, who will follow the trail to find out what clues they may have left along the way in order to uncover their secrets. The opportunists take advantage of this information to discover the procedures used to win the *Kussunde.* This way, they'll be able to beat them; what's more, they sleep together on top of the house, but in a dispersed way; they sleep in one place so that none of them can betray them by uncovering their secrets.

In the evening, after the first caravan of people from different *tabankas* arrives to watch the *kussunde*, the dany *kussunde* group, made up exclusively of women, performs their dangas to excite and attract the attention of the spectators. This group dances so that people can see among themselves who is the most beautiful or who wears the most beautiful costumes, hairstyles and ornaments. They dance until 3 a.m., then there is a break at 5 a.m. for the *dany kussunde* to take a shower, and they resume at 8 a.m. in the morning. When they have finished, they then go in search of the group of *n'ghaies,* since "[...] the *n'hae* (*n'ghaies*) of each village are given the role of preparing the songs and dangas that will be performed during the festival by groups of young people from the different villages, in an artistic challenge, each trying to win and assert their superiority." (CAMMILLERI, 2010, p. 66).

In addition, on the first day of *Kussunde*, in the afternoon, around 1pm, the nghaies begin their disputes. The *nghaies* dance is the one that the whole *tabanka* awaits with great expectation, liveliness, euphoria and anxiety, although different groups take part in this dance, "[...] where the spectators, moved to tears, musically mix their solugos with the chants." (ZEMP, 2013, p. 46). On the occasion of the *Kussunde,* to find out the winning group, they are usually ranked by the number of people who go after one of the groups of *n'ghaies.* Both the best *Kussunde* singers and the most renowned dangarinos are ranked by *tabankas*, based on the different *Kussunde* they have participated in. It should also be emphasized that other GuiC-Bissau people, as well as foreigners, cannot actively participate in these dangas, but only as spectators.

The *Kussunde* dangarinos carry the white cloth flag that symbolizes peace, because there is often confusion and chaos among the spectators. This flag is also used to signal the start of the competition, which is enthusiastically participated in by the spectators. When the groups of dangarinos go to start the *Kussunde,* they usually place this flag where they actually dangle the *Kussunde.* Next,

> The most extravagant costumes began to appear, including criangas smeared with mud and sporting beards in imitation of old men. In the groups that follow one another, the best dangarinos or dangarinas and the best singers stand out. One young man stands out for using a cow's horn from which he can extract musical sounds. [Each group, under the guidance of a leader, will try to surprise everyone with

> innovations in music, costume and choreography. On the day of the competition, the gifts awarded to the best are placed in the center of the yard, with a container of water next to it to quench the dangarinos' thirst. (KIPP, 2005, p. 1).

It's worth emphasizing that, before the *Kussunde* begins, each *n'ghaie* shows off their skills to the spectators. During the dance, due to the crowds of spectators, some of them climb trees in order to get a good view of the synchronized movements of the dangarinos. The day after the first act, the *m'pebe* group dances. In the same way, all the *n'ghies-only* groups that compete are usually prepared and convinced to convince the audience, because it is the spectators who obviously serve as arbiters and decide, at the end of the show, which *tabanka* has won over *Kussunde*.

Each group of dangarinos has between 25 and 30 members and each group sings between 15 and 20 songs, mainly about the daily life of the tabanka; always repeating them constantly, while the spectators always improvise these songs very easily, even though they are usually new songs, sung on the occasion of the dance. The *kussunde,* which takes place over four consecutive days, has two decisive days, namely the day it begins and the day it ends, when the winning group is chosen. During these days, the hosts offer pork, chicken and goat dishes, as well as drinks to the spectators. These offerings will be reciprocated when they go to dango in their *tabanka*. The same amount of pigs and chickens that they sacrifice in that *tabanka* for them will also be reciprocated by the same participants, since every group gives something to their colleagues who are taking part in the dance. The group hosting the *tabanka* provides all these things because they raise the money needed for it.

Finally, what can actually delay the performance of this dance is the death of someone in the *moransa,* "out of respect for tradition"[16] ; before that, nothing can delay this dance-party, apart from impediments considered to be divine or of ancestral origin. In this case, everything is postponed until the year when there is a good rice harvest. At the time of the danga, the dangarinos hold ploughs representing the cultivation of rice, and also symbolizing that they are skilled rice farmers. In addition, they have brooms which symbolically serve to sweep away the dirt in the *tabanka*, in other words, to put an end to the evil that is within it and to stop illicit practices such as adultery, selfishness, opportunism, among others. With regard to the pistols, the weapons and the tergado, they symbolize that the *tabanka* has the means to defend itself against the enemy; thus, they dangam simulating that they are doing something, executing their synchronized movements. In fact, during the dance, each group does everything to attract the attention of the people who come to watch. At the dance site, the

[16] According to N'sab Namara, interview granted in July 2015 by video call.

group of *n'ghaies* dangles and maneuvers in the containers placed at the dance site and the spectators stand around watching. So they do whatever it takes to win the danga. Fortunato (2015, p. 1) pointed out that:

> [...] the Balanta party is based on many colors, the rhythm of the drums, the rattle of the ornaments, and sometimes the lyrics of the songs, simple and repetitive [...] the dangarino dances pretending to be drunk, provoking laughter and clapping. There is no shortage of 'clowns' at the party, who, painted white, try to make people laugh with nonsensical dangas and other antics. The "stage" where the dangas take place is open to anyone who wants to take part [...] The party is also a place for the dangarinos to show off their new hairstyles. In addition, they wear tall hats made of tassels made of yarn in many colors on their heads and all kinds of adornments on their bodies, from chains around their necks to rubber straps on their bravos or hanging around their waists. But also necklaces of green branches, leather or rope, bracelets of beads, sticks, axes and machetes in their hands [...] but everything is part of the performance, even when the ground shakes with their synchronized jumping [...] (PEIXEIRO, 2012, p. 1).

Figure 4 - Group of *N'ghaies* dangling *Kussunde* over the container

Source: Lallalleiro (2008)[1] .

Figure 5 - Flow of people on the occasion of *Kussunde* [17][18]

Source: Lallalleiro (2008)[18]

In *Kussunde,* the competing groups sing indirectly to people alluding to illicit or immoral things that they have done or are used to doing in the *tabanka,* especially if a person has committed adultery or participated in a certain crime. They do this because, for the Brasa, these things are shameful and disgusting. It's worth emphasizing that the Brasa are better known for this dance than for others, because it's the one that has spread the most within the national territory of Guinea. Authors who have written about the identity of the Brasa people have always mentioned this dance in their works, identifying it, however, as just a party; however, it is obvious that these dangas are not just parties, but dangas accompanied by parties.

In fact, it's important to note that "kussunde is also the name of an instrument used to play and dango Brocksa, and is one of the most used instruments in all traditional Balanta festivals and throughout the region inhabited by this ethnic group".[19] The *Kussunde* instruments are two drums[20] , a smaller *bumbulum*[21] (talking drum) and the ram's horn as a wind instrument. Since ancient times, the Brasa have sung *Kussunde* without a microphone and danced on top of the pilao (which is a narrow object that is more difficult to maneuver, and where there is not enough space to maneuver), communicating to perform it through the *bumbulum* talking drum. Furthermore, the *bumbulum* has a significant value in the life of the Brasa; through it they communicate with people from other *tabankas* to take part in any event; it also serves to announce funeral ceremonies in the *tabanka.* Cavalcante and Jesus (2012, p.

[17] Available at: <http://lallalleiro.blogspot.com.br/2008/06/kusunde.html>. Accessed on: 07 Aug. 2015.
[18] Available at: <http://lallalleiro.blogspot.com.br/2008/06/kusunde.html>. op. cit.
[19]Interview given by Sia Namara on Facebook in September 2015.
[20] The drum is made from the poilao in which it is dug; it is usually decorated with goatskin, and ropes are also put on it to hold the leather used.
[21] It is built with a poilao tree and dug from the inside.

200) say: "when man plays, he is totally inserted into the [speaking] drum, or vice versa"; therefore, in Brasa society "the drum does not disassociate itself from the rhythm and the rhythm does not disassociate itself from the person or from the circularity of the universe around it" (CAVALCANTE; JESUS, 2012, p. 202-203). Nowadays, the spectacle is communicated on the radio when it is about to take place.

Another instrument used is a kind of sound clamp tied to the pds, known as a *kiseita.* In the past they used to use a milk can, inserting a shard of a bottle into it. This procedure is no longer used because of the wounds it causes to the dangarinos' pds. In addition, the dangarinos use sheep horn painted in different colors to decorate themselves. Both the *N'Ghaies* and the *Dany Kussude* put tin cans on their bodies and stick pebbles in them to attract people's attention. Dangarinos also use mosaics (but they cut them off part by part) as body adornment.

Nowadays, tiles are used in the bragos by the *N'Ghaies.* When they dance, they use a loudspeaker and a microphone to sing. They also use the *siko,* an instrument that is now often used because it makes a more pleasant sound. It used to be difficult to hire *siko* experts, but since the beginning of the year 2000, *siko* has been used more than *bumbulum* and other drums. It's clear that the *bumbulum* needs people to listen to it, because people speak through it. However, few people still manage to decipher the message that comes out of it, because there has been a lack of interest and contempt on the part of some people for learning this language, which is considered to be unbecoming of people who consider themselves educated and modern.

Simoes (1935, p. 118) points out that "once the blufo [blufu bindag][22] has made a public declaration of his love, in the kussunde circle [...] he meets the [girl's] father, to whom he conveys his wishes and hands over the goods mentioned." In fact, this has to do with the request for courtship, so that she can get married, because the ancients and ancients demand that the young people of the *tabanka* who don't yet have boyfriends make the declaration at the *kussunde.* The *N'ghaies,* for their part, take advantage of this moment to propose to the parents of the girls they want.

The performance of the *Kussunde* shows survival as a sign of gratitude for the Iras, in order to provide the *tabankas* with plenty, since "[...] the land is synonymous with the survival of the group, consolidating its identity in relation to other groups." (HANDEM, 1986, p. 57). Furthermore, the *Kussunde* is subsistence and a means of relating to the land and restitution to the ancestors, since the land "[...] marks the internal authority of its chief and the recognition of this authority by the outside." (HANDEM, 1986, p. 57). Additionally,

[22] My emphasis.

> [...] the earth, and in particular the tusks in our case, is a natural and spiritual entity on a cosmological level. It is the source of life and the lakes that man weaves with it necessarily pass through the mediation of the genii and ancestors from whom its powerful fecundity originates. That is why it is not possible to appropriate it as if it were an object." (IMBALI, 1992, p. 15).

It's clear that the *Kussunde* dance is also a religious sacrifice dedicated to the Iras, because of their complacency, their protection and their interest in the *tabankas*, since they make sure that there is an abundance of rice. In these terms, abundance is symbolic and the result of hard human work to survive in this earthly life, always in harmony with the divine. In addition, "the land gives rise to recognition of the group's legitimacy by the living, but also by the ancestors and the spirits, insofar as the person who acquires it and makes it bear fruit establishes a pact of protection with these religious entities." (HANDEM, 1986 p. 57-58). The *Kussunde* was also "performed with a very precise objective and, at the same time, was the product of exuberance; it was completely spontaneous and came from a desire to have fun." (KEALIINOHOMOKU, 2013, p. 124). On the other hand, it also aims to "[...] facilitate the sustainability of the adepts who came from neighboring villages to attend the event"[23] . Therefore, "[...] land is a good whose value is a function of the relationship that man establishes with it". (IMBALI, 1992, p. 15).

3.2 END OF ACTIVITIES

At the end of all the *Kussunde* dance activities, the winning group divides up the prizes they've won, which are made available by the *tabanka* groups, who pool their resources for this purpose. Some of these prizes are given in the form of money and others are given in the form of animals, such as goats, pigs, chickens and others. If the animals they've been given aren't enough for them, they buy new ones in order to hold a big party to rejoice as a team.

[24]These statements are in line with the following reflections: "at the end, the groups divide the prizes among themselves and, when part of the prizes is given in cash, they buy animals to hold a group party" (KIPP, 2005, p. 1)[25] . The women then have to continue their

[23] Interview granted in July 2015 via Facebook.
[24] The author also mentioned that the groups are divided [...], but in the *kussunde* dance it's only one team that wins.
[25] Available at: <http://senegambia.blogspot.com.br/2005/08/guin-bissau-aspectos-da-vida-de-um_19.html>.

dany kussunde activities until it's time to accompany the n *'ghaies.*

Finally, it should be noted that:

> [...] a young man [...] stands out by using a cow horn from which he can extract musical sounds. But it is the last groups, the older ones - the Ngwai (girls) and the Nunkuman (boys) - who put on the best shows. They, dressed in straw and adorned with mirrors, and they, excellent players and dangarinos, amaze those watching and end up winning the best prizes. (KIPP, 2005, p. 1).

The statements: "the Ngwai *[n'guatch]* for the girls and the Nunkuman *[n'kuman*] for the boys - who put on the best shows [...] and end up winning the best prizes." are in line with what I found in my own ethnographic research. That's why I disagree, because both the *n'kuman* and the *n'guatch* don't win prizes, but the *n'ghaies* do. Therefore, when the dance is over, each group is usually escorted to the *moransa* where they have family or friends to sleep. If one of them has a friend in the same *tabanka,* they go to sleep at his house; if one or more of them has nowhere else to stay, the people in the *tabanka* where they watch *Kussunde* usually take them in. In the evening, they eat some leftovers and leave for their homes the next day.

3.3 REFLECTIONS ON THE CHANGES IN KUSSUNDE

Currently, the *Kussunde* has undergone some changes in terms of how the request is made. For example, if neighboring people from other *tabankas* are going to participate in the *Kussunde,* the *tabanka* interested in competing takes the flag placed at the site of the dance as a sign of making the request for the *Kussunde* in the year when there is an abundance of rice. However, this procedure will only take place with the confirmation and authorization of the elders, as mentioned above.

Between 1970 and 1999 or so, *Kussunde* was danced from 1pm to 7pm; however, in view of some discussions and claims by some people that if they started dangling early, they would actually win the *Kussunde*, because they would dangle much longer, favoring their victory. With this in mind, they changed the time from 11 a.m. to 7 p.m., but this varies from *tabanka to tabanka.* On the occasion of *Kussunde,* in order to be more popular, the Dangarinos use *n'ghol.*

There were no security guards to keep order and, when there was intrigue and disorder among the spectators, it was the old men who tried to control the riots. Nowadays, there are security guards for this work, called *n'kumam*, who also dangam, although they play a minor role in the danga itself. They are considered to be "community policemen of the *tabankas"*

Accessed on: 07 Aug. 2015.

because they maintain order and keep an eye on the danga site .[26]

In recent times, there have been major changes within *Kussunde:* there are *Kussunde* that are danced in the same *tabanka* and there are *Kussunde* that are danced between *tabankas*, as I mentioned earlier. In the past, *Kussunde* used to be performed exclusively in *moransas* of a particular *tabanka* for the competition. And since around 2000, there have been groups that wear the uniforms of troops, others imitate refugees, representing the wars that are happening in the world and the desperation of people seeking refuge. In the same vein, there are also groups made up of men who wear scary plastic masks symbolizing the terror of sorcery caused by evil people in the *morass*. It's a warning to people to understand that they should no longer carry out this nefarious practice.

In the past, people who belonged to one of the groups didn't dare go without dangar; however, nowadays, they break the established rules and don't receive the punishment because they consider themselves educated and modern, which is why they have a preconceived view of *Kussunde*. In the past, the people of the *tabankas* saw these dangas as something very important and of great impact on society. However, nowadays, in view of so-called modernity, the stereotyped view of many people has grown, that is, influences from outside mean that people don't take *Kussunde* seriously, while others look down on it, devaluing this dance and calling it a "primitive" dance, practiced and performed by so-called uncivilized and perverse people.

It's clear that such statements are preconceived ideas and stereotyped by some people who don't even have the perception, the vision or the notion of how this dance is practiced among these people. Instead of paying enough attention to it to be able to understand the techniques that the dangarinos use, they reinforce an ethnocentric and preconceived idea. Because of the influence from outside, the *tabankas* who dang *Kussunde*, we have seen that some costumes are being considered obsolete and dangar with shoes is gaining a huge space in this dance. In the past, the *N'ghaies* danced *Kussunde* barefoot. It is also common today to use *siko* string instruments and plastic masks to terrorize people, as I mentioned earlier; these elements were not used before. However, nowadays they are gaining a lot of ground in this dance and people simply don't follow the rules that were previously established for it. Some people from outside the *tabanka*, who are actually taking part in these dangas, are having a big influence on the disappearance and imperceptibility of many of the cultural elements mentioned above. The clothes of these people, in turn, are being seen as a model to follow on the occasion of this dance, to the detriment of the clothes that the dangarinos wore beforehand.

[26] Interview by video call, July 2015.

The dangarinos built a mud plane and danced on top of it to compete.[27] This plane is used to represent life after death, in other words, the destiny that is the continuity of life in eternity.

"If dance has played a fundamental role in human evolution [...] it can always be used to regenerate social life and to allow people to recover [or regain] their senses." (YOUNGERMAN, 2013, p. 84). It can be said that the Brasa youth should continue to dance the *Kussunde*, because it is very essential in their lives and is part of their culture; in this way, they are spreading sets of the values of their people and their consequences and impacts on society, because the dance has served them well,

> [...] it serves to help develop a more general appreciation of human artistic values, and should therefore be considered educationally [as indeed it was, and still is, in many African societies]. The future of dance as a democratic artistic activity rests on our educational system [in this case in the United States, but also in Brasa society][28] [...]. Only when dance is conceived communally will it be able to exert a full cultural influence (H'DOUBLER, 1957, apud YOUNGERMAN, 2013, p. 85).

Nowadays, the women comb their hair, wear chokers, sunglasses, make up their faces, also wear human hair and mega, and perfume their bodies, while the men wear tight jeans, sneakers and perfume their bodies to serve as decorations on the occasion of *Kussunde*. The costumes of the Dangarinos, for their part, have undergone many changes, although they continue to wear Bijago skirts.

[27] Interview by video call, Aug. 2015.
[28] My emphasis.

4 KANTA PO AND ITS DYNAMICS

Kanta Po means *rib filack* in the Brasa language, or literally 'cantar pau' in Portuguese. It's a competitive dance performed exclusively by the *blufu bindag* that make up a particular *tabanka*. It is done when they are about to go to the *fanado.*

According to the popular narrative, *Kanta Po* arose from an argument between two childhood friends who said to each other: "I have more singing ability than you". They actually had this argument at the *n'ghaie* stage and decided to compete when they went to the fanado to see who would win, but in the end they drew. However, it was a duel that really stuck in people's memories, because on that day the spectators saw unbelievable things in terms of the songs sung and the dance performed, since on the same day the competitors sang and performed a hitherto unknown dance[29] , in which they displayed supernatural powers. Both contestants possessed extraordinary powers and were supported by family members and friends with supernatural powers who effectively contributed to the contest so that one of them could win[30] . Thus, the clash became a competitive dance that could fascinate the audience and the *tabanka* at the same time. Each *tabanka* shows off its potential by trying to scare the *tabankas* who might want to belittle them, i.e. scare the people who might slander that *moransa*, seeing it as useless. It used to be a dispute between two *blufu bindag*, but now it's a competition between many *blufu bindag* within the same *tabanka.*

It is the ancients and ancients of the *tabanka* who organize the *Kanta Po* dance. In August, the elders send *Blufu Bindag* to cut the fictitious stick, since they are responsible for making it and burying it. On the night they cut this stick, the elder in charge of the *fram* pours the bordao cane over it to announce the date of *Kanta Po*. However, they don't necessarily sing it the same year they cut it. When they set a certain date, if a tragedy happens (the death of a person in the *tabanka)* they postpone the dance to another year. However, if there is still a week to go if someone dies, even a member of the Community Body[31] , they don't postpone the *Kanta Po*.

Kanta Po takes place specifically in a *tabanka* and each *tabanka* has three or more groups. They start singing it in November and continue until March, when the rehearsal days are added together. Despite the rehearsal days, this dance lasts four consecutive days and they don't perform it in one place, they perform it in different places in the same *tabanka.* As far as *Kanta Po* rehearsals are concerned, they only take place at night, just like *Kussunde* and

[29] Interview given by N'sab Namara in July 2015 via video call.
[30] Idem.
[31] Interview granted in Guinea-Bissau during my stay there in 2013.

Broska, because of the dangarinos' activities during the day. During the rehearsal, the people of the *tabanka* participate en masse. If they set a date for the Kanta Po, each group that is going to compete raises money to buy pigs, goats, sheep, chickens, wine, juices, rice and other food for the participants who have come from different places. It's customary for the ancients to tell the dangarinos in their *moransa* to do whatever they want to win the *Kanta Po,* including making a pact with Iras, because then they'll settle everything.

Kanta Po starts at 12pm and finishes at 6pm on four consecutive days. In order to know who has really won the competition, they dangle it non-stop. The willingness to dangle is immense, as it brings reputation, popularity and privileges. These notorieties have repercussions in every region of the country where *Kanta Po* is danced. It is important to say that "The people who danced [and dangle][32] within a community generally shared [and share] kinship, residential space, occupation, religion and social status, as well as being born, as it were, into the same repertoire of dances and ways of moving." (BUCKLAND, 2013, p. 147). Thus, it can be said that the dangarinos *blufu bindag* are from the same *tabanka* and a person from another *tabanka* cannot participate, let alone something from another people, whether from GuiC-Bissau or from other countries.

On their occasion, all the *blufu bindag* wear animal hides as masks, such as wolf and cow hides, and hold a horse or cow tail in their hand, literally in the Brasa language *kibanfe ni falalas, kabanfe ni nhare*, to make bazofia. These tails are prepared by a diviner through a ritual that gives them supernatural powers, so that the person who possesses them can become famous. The tails of these animals symbolize strength, reputation and vital energy. During the act, the dangarinos maneuver them from side to side, as a way of making their opponents fear them; the dangarinos are fearless, as they are endowed with exceptional bravery and courage. What's more, Dangarinos wear malilas on their feet, plastic slingbacks, buzio, aluminum to serve as body adornment. They also use animal horns, because it is through them that they communicate and extract the sounds they sing.

The musical instruments of *Kanta Po* are the *siko,* which effectively became a new instrument in this dance, in which they also play three[33][34] drums, namely a small one, a normal one and a large one. From what we can see, *Kanta Po* hasn't changed much in terms of instruments, since only the flute and the *siko* have been introduced. Nowadays, it is performed on the radio, but in the past it was done using the *bumbulum*, which is the means of communication for getting the message across.

---

[32] My emphasis.

[33] It is built with a blood stick (like a tree), which is then hollowed out using goatskin. When playing the drum, two sticks are held to play it in order to get different rhythms; it is carried in a diagonal position.

[34] Available at: <http://tchogue.blogspot.pt/>. Accessed on: July 20, 2016.

Figure 6 - The bumbulum talking drum

Source: IBD .[34]

During the dance, the groups sometimes huddle together to compete. Each competing group then has a leader. If one of the leaders runs off, the people with him follow. There are also always hundreds of people of different age groups, both from the same *tabanka* and from different places, taking part and running with him. What's more, each competitor has their coadjuvant, who helps them when they sing, known as the Brasa de *al ta many ma des,* "[...] the groups in competition, who sing and dango [...] It's really just a leader and two or three helpers, who sing and dango." (PEIXEIRO, 2012, p. 1)[35] . On the other hand, each leader of the *Kanta Po* group only appears when his group has a significant number of target audiences. When he appears, his members take him to a gigantic tree so that people can see him, because people are waiting for this magical moment. However, they don't leave him there for long and, after he comes down, they hide him; there are people who take care of these protagonists at this very important moment, both for him and for the rest of his team.

According to popular belief, some leaders go into the sea on the occasion of the dance, then dive in for thirty seconds and come out with a caiman. With feats like this, the target audience is enchanted and the dance gains more crowds. In the *Kanta Po* dance, Ira is incorporated into the stick that has been cut down in the forest by the *blufu binddg*, and this, in turn, gives supernatural power to the person who is going to possess it. This person, with the

[35] Available at: <http://noticias.sapo.mz/lusa/artigo/14523933.html>. Accessed on: 03 May 2016.

help of Iras, can win the competition. There are people who are capable of doing anything to win such a competition, which is why some *tabanka* people with supernatural abilities instigate and entice their friends and neighbors to give them the most important things, for example: their children, a loved one, and so on, so that the person can win the *Kanta Po,* because it is believed that, in order to win this competition, people have to make a pact with Iras. There are people with supernatural powers who convince Iras in order to win *Kanta Po*. When this dance is over, it is believed that these people can win and leave a legacy and then die, because it is believed that at the time of making the contract, or rather the pact with *Trds*[36] , some people tell him that if they win the competition, he can kill them later. The important thing for them is to leave a legacy.

On this occasion, some accept the challenge, since the most important thing for them is to be famous and this fame will be passed on by word of mouth and generation after generation; moreover, winning the *Kanta Poë* for the Brasa is a privilege that is accessible to only a few, which is why people do whatever it takes to win it. In this sense, each dangarino makes different pacts with Iras, because there is a great deal of competition during this dance in whichever Brasa *tabanka* the *Kanta Po* takes place in.

In addition, some dangarinos go secretly to ask for help from a very brave elder, in order to obtain the fictitious stick, since this is not just any object; therefore this "stick is a sacred object, which the 'big men' go secretly to fetch from the forest and which will be there on feast days, without anyone knowing where". (PEIXEIRO, 2012, p. 1). The people who first populate a *tabanka* have more power over this fictitious stick. In fact, they are more likely to win the danga because they know the *tabanka* where they live well and already have some intimacy with its Iras. This makes it easier for them to take advantage of the Iras or convince them in relation to the others. However, this doesn't mean that others can't do the same. There are also powerful people who convince Iras to help them get the fictitious stick.

It's important to emphasize that the ranking of the dangarinos is done because of the commitment and skill displayed in different competitions in relation to this dance, and the spectators who, in effect, give credit to the dangarinos. In this way, they are boasted about by the whole *tabanka* of the Brasa, i.e. the achievements of the dangarinos are exalted by the people present at the dance. Through their efforts, they are known by the other regions of GuiC-Bissau, gaining popularity and fame. In fact, spectators use the different achievements of different dangas to select the winners of this dance's names, in order to classify both dancers and singers. In this way, their name is exalted and they gain fame to the point where they are

[36]Interview with different Guinean immigrants (brasa) in Sao Paulo (Brazil) in Dec. 2015.

classified by the spectators as the best during the moment in which they stand out. The winner of this competition is the person who has the largest number of people following them, just like in the *Kussunde* dance.

In their performance, every step the *blufu binddg* take is related to showing off to people that they are powerful people. Their celebration, however, aims to make people understand that, within that village, there are super-powerful people, endowed with powers that naturally don't let them succumb to the mediocrity of life, as they try to overcome human limits through the cosmogonies that enable them to understand the universe.

Its performance is often a real mess when it comes to the magic that the dangarinos perform in front of the audience, since during the dance the dangarinos dangle in an abnormal way through jumping, booing and the execution of different movements that the spectators dictate. In this way, *Kanta Po* provides an extra-human dimension in line with the *Irds.*

The vital energy is inherent in *Kanta Po* through its resonance of a greater amplitude of vibration and the return of something of joy that they feel for the ancestors. On its occasion, people see incredible and amazing things that are inherent to an atheistic force, as the *blufu bindag* at *Kanta Po* try to overcome human limits that life imposes on them. Consequently, in *Kanta Po* there is always a duel between divinity and social balance. In other words, between human and divine strength, because the people who dance do things beyond the ordinary and transform themselves. In the course of the dance, the spectators see the dangarinos as unusual people, since the dangarinos show more skills through the magic they perform in front of the dance, doing things they didn't do before. Facts like these impress people and enchant them even more. *Kanta Po* also tries to instill in people values such as courage, joy, the struggle to break through life's obstacles and vital energy, which is fundamental for maintaining earthly and cosmic life.

In general, *Kanta Po* makes its audience more attracted and also enchants the dangarinos. Its dominance in terms of imagination, aesthetics, the inner and outer world is fundamental in the lives of Dangarinos, since it is in consonance with divinity, since for the Brasa everything is directed towards divinities and ancestry. The *Kanta Po* is done to show the supernatural power that the Dangarinos possess and serves to frighten each other. In this dance, the Dangarinos show that they are super-powerful and powerful in relation to others. Since its inception, the Brasa have considered *Kanta Po to* be a challenge of strength with the aim of showing who has the most supernatural powers. And to this day, the conception of *Kanta Po* has continued and has a great impact on the Brasa.

For Africans in general and the Brasa in particular, the relationship between man and nature, between the divine and the human is intrinsic and inwardly profound. What's more, the elements of nature are endowed with divine powers, which is certainly also reflected in the *Kanta Po* dance through the movements that the dangarinos perform. Let's take a look at this interpretation below: "The purpose of this form of intimate relationship is to achieve and maintain a harmonious balance between man and the universe." (DOMINGOS, 2011, p. 2). This dance is seen among these people as a great display of extra-human powers, because people see unusual things in the Dangarinos. As mentioned above, in relation to all the cultural manifestations that take place within the same group, in Kanta Po people do unbelievable things for the glory and fame of their *tabanka.* In addition, it should be noted that,

> *Kanta* Po has these two important moments. The days it lasts begin with dozens of competitors parading in a vast square marked off by spectators. The fight then takes place, two by two, anywhere in the square.
> field, in the middle of a lot of dust but without judges or referees. You win what you get knock the other down and their back touches the ground (PEIXEIRO, 2012, p. 1).

At this dance, the young people usually have various entertainments, among them: Brasa wrestling, which is a form of brawling in terms of entertainment, in which young people and teenagers fight in order to find out who fights well, i.e. who has the best strategy.
in these fights. Those who don't dance do it as a way of impressing more audiences, so that they feel more excited, and don't just watch *Kanta Po* dance. You could say that: "although synonymous with solidarity and fraternization, "Canta Po" *[Kanta Po]* brings together hundreds of people who watch wrestling among the younger generation [...]" (PEIXEIRO, 2012, p. 1).

Figure 7 - N'ghaies fighting in the *Kanta Po* act

Source: Lallalleiro (2008) .[37]

On the last day of the dance, the sacred stick invisibly returns to the forest and no one knows when, because it is the secret of the elders. (PEIXEIRO, 2012, p. 1). Furthermore, the fieticio stick is a supernatural and sacred "invisible" stick, in the sense that it is a secret among the ancients who actually know how it works (PEIXEIRO, 2012, p. 1). In this dance, unlike the *Kussunde*, there is usually "no prize for the winners, only a gain in prestige. Just as there is no humiliation for the loser, but recognition for courage and merit as a worthy adversary." (SIGA, 2015, p. 55). It's worth pointing out that the author of the following quote made a mistake, because he used it to cover all the dangas carried out by the Brasa, although the quote is restricted to *Kanta Po*.

> In general, there are always results that may favor one party or the other, or even a draw. It's worth noting that sometimes there is a debate about who won the challenge, but in the end there is a consensus on the result. The great judges Available at:<http://lallalleiro.blogspot.com.br/2008/06/kusunde.html>. Accessed on: 07 Aug. 2015. all of this ends up being the people or groups who are not an active part of the activity, but who have come to take part as spectators. It is up to them to decide the best performance of the competitors (SIGA, 2015, p. 55).

Initially, the Amphritrians only made food during *Kanta Po* for people for whom they had some affection and sympathy as a way of showing their benevolence towards them. Nowadays, instead, they make and distribute the food to everyone who attends the dance.

Kanta Po is usually performed infrequently, a fact which means that it is "currently almost disappearing in Guinean society." (PEIXEIRO, 2012, p. 1), especially in Brasa society, since it is considered a sacred dance and is only performed by people with supernatural powers, which is why it takes time to know how it is danced.

In addition, *Kanta Po* is rarely performed, because there is a considerable waste of money in this dance, specifically rice, because they spend a lot of money hiring soothsayers who are usually with them on this occasion to help them win the competition. They also waste a lot of rice making food for the spectators. Nowadays, however, the Brasa sell the rice instead of using it in the dango festivals (IMBALI, 1992, p. 14). Since "[...] today the Balantas have a different view of commercial activity, practicing it more and more." (IMBALI, 1992, p. 15). Previously, "for the Balantas, trading meant the pursuit of individual wealth. This was contrary to the rules of their society. Their society rejected or simply marginalized anyone who tried it." (IMBALI, 1992, p. 12). For this reason, the Brasa economy didn't develop for a long time, as people lived solely off rice. In addition, it is clear that their activities have operated without money for many years (IMBALI, 1992, p. 12).

In light of this, Faustino Imbali stated that:

> [...] the Kanta Po festival has not been held in the Tombali region for more than ten years. As for the Kisunde festival, it no longer has the same frequency or impact among young people. These two festivals involve a great deal of expenditure on rice after the fanado festival. The general opinion of the people of the area, of all ages, is very pessimistic about the future of these festivals (IMBALI, 1992, p. 14).

In addition, *Kanta Po* occurs infrequently because it is considered to be a dance that brings about many disagreements and disputes between *moransa*, since during its preparations, during the four-month period, no one dares to go to the other *moransa*. If a person goes to the other *moransa*, they can be considered a spy, i.e. they can be accused of having gone there to do something to harm the group, for example by observing their frank points. Anyone going to the rival *moransa*, or indeed to the opposing *moransa*, could result in a beating or a severe beating.

Although, when this dance is over, friendships continue as before and other people, for their part, always harbor resentment in the event of a beating or a loss in the dance, since they are not satisfied with the defeat they have suffered or the beating they have received if they happen to be the opposing *moransa* at the time of the rehearsal. Faced with this fact, the ancients of the other *tabankas* try to mobilize their young people to stop this dance, since it brings enmity *to the tabankas;* so they perform some symbolic ceremonies to be able to replace *Kanta Po* and then perform the *fanado.*

Despite the fact that many *tabankas* are trying to put an end to this dance, others still do it with great insistence, because, according to them, *Kanta Po is* a dance that is part of their culture and it can't just stop overnight, because if they didn't perform *Kanta Po,* they would be belittling their culture and also contributing to its disappearance, and the next generation would never know what *Kanta* Po is and would not sing it, nor would they know its importance and its impact on the Brasa, which is why they perform it incessantly.

4.1 REFLECTIONS ON THE CHANGES IN KANTA PO

Brasa converts to the Christian religion, especially in evangelical churches, abandon not only the *Kanta Po* dance, but also the others, because for them they are "primitive", "satanic" or "demonic" practices, while Catholic Brasa don't have such prejudiced ideas about them, and some of them practice these dances without any problem. It's important to point out that *Kanta Po* is certainly not danced out of thin air; people dangle it for a specific purpose, which is to show off their powers. Of course, "many dangas, and also songs, have a pronounced 'sacred' character and can only be understood in relation to cosmogonical representations: the dangas of the initiates, consecrated to the divinity of the ancestors [...]" (ZEMP, 2013, p. 49).

On the other hand, "from an anthropological point of view, there is no such thing as a 'primitive dance'. There are dangas performed by so-called "primitive" peoples, but these are too diverse to correspond to a stereotype." (CAMARGO, 2013, p. 18). Moreover, from the same point of view [...] all dangas are ethnic, because all dangas reflect the cultural traditions within which they were developed." (CAMARGO, 2013, p. 17). Therefore, "ethnic danga" should represent a form of danga belonging to a particular group of people, sharing genetic, linguistic and cultural lakes [...] (KEALIINOHOMOKU, 2013, p. 139). These facts are really what *Kanta Po* represents in terms of its structuring principle.

Some influences from outside the *tabanka*[3] are harming the dance, because if a person from the urban center goes there without wearing the customary costumes, they can effectively influence other people not to wear them, as is always the case. On the other hand, some innovations that are being made are obviously contributing significantly to the enrichment of this dance for the benefit of the Brasa. Among them, we highlight the following: currently, the groups that dango *Kanta Po* bring *m'beletchu.* Naturally, they usually bring *m'beletchu* not only in *Kanta Po,* but also in *Kussunde.*

They also bring *murrus* (soothsayers) to captivate and help them gain popularity. In this dance, there used to be no fortune-teller to favor or harm anyone; however, nowadays people resort to different ways in order to win, as mentioned above. Faced with countless demands, there is often betrayal between people in the same *moransa* in terms of informing opponents of their secrets as a way of destabilizing the group. To prevent this from happening, the elders arrange to go to the *baloba* to warn *Iras* to liquidate the person who dares to disappoint the group and, beforehand, they inform people about the trip to the *baloba*.

Therefore, if a person betrays the group by telling their opponents their routes and their secrets, in other words, unveiling the pact that they surely made with Iras to win *Kanta Po*, that person will die, as is popularly believed. In this case, the groups keep a close eye on their food and water to avoid sabotage. This infidelity happens because of the affinity that the people in the *tabanka* have with another, and sometimes people betray the group by giving away pertinent information in order to settle their debt, or by revealing the secrets of the person or the team in order to get something in return; they do this for personal gain, which is why the ancients take this initiative in order to prevent them from defrauding the *moransa*'s expectations, since winning *Kanta Po* is very prestigious for the *tabanka.*

5 BROSKA AND ITS DYNAMICS

Broska is a popular Brasa dance style, which is performed among young people of different ages who don't perform nuptials or circumcision in order to strengthen fraternal friendships within this people. In terms of its creation, *Broskaë* is more recent than *Kussunde* and *Kanta Po* and is now as popular as the other dangas, since it was created by the *bamakite* group, literally "those who came" (the original term is *bumakite*, literally in Brasa "we who came"). And people began to call this group *bamakite.* It was founded in Ntchate in 1977, through a joke between the young people of that *tabanka* in which they danced and sang, at the same time laughing at each other for the way they danced and sang. The word *Broska* comes from the term *roskana* in Brasa, literally "rubbing the feet on the floor", since the *Bamakite* group danced as a form of entertainment by rubbing their feet on the floor. In this sense, over time, this entertainment came to be called *Broska;* furthermore, "This dance was baptized with the name of Broksa, [...] after independence in the village of NtcliaN by the Balantas in eastern GuiC-Bissau"[37] . Domingos Sanha, known as Domingos *Broska,* also known as *Broska*'s uncle, one of *Broska*'s singers, always mentions this group, and in one of his songs he called them the "lords *of Broska".*

Broska is usually done when there is a host girl among the Brasa youth. In this regard, there are usually different competitors with the aim of convincing her to date and get married in the middle of this *tabanka or moransa.* It also happens when a farmer brings people from other *tabankas* to work in his field or rice paddy, i.e. this dance takes place when there is hard work in the same *tabanka.* When they have finished this tiring task, the young people who live there, in turn, call each other to organize a rejoicing party about the act of dancing. On this occasion, on the last day of agricultural work, the *Broska* dance is organized to show appreciation for the work done, thus thanking the farmers who obviously helped them carry out the task of growing rice, which is a very essential act for the Brasa. The hosts do everything they can to please the people who are going to take part in the rice cultivation by organizing the *Broska* dance*; during* this dance, pigs, goats and chickens are sacrificed and a large amount of food is cooked for both those who are dancing and those who are not actively taking part; during this dance, people drink, eat and celebrate. Each *tabanka* and *moransa* shows its strength and potential in terms of the dance. The *Broska* is also a competition for the *tabankas* to show their values and identities to the other non-Brasa regions.

Another reason why young men organize this dance is that there are times when it's

[37] Interview given by Nhafe Camargo in July 2015, via video call.

impossible to see their girlfriends; so they organize it as a way of being able to see them, because they go to their *tabankas* to get some of their belongings, and they end up going there to retrieve their things. The boyfriends, in turn, take advantage of this moment to organize the *Broska.* They start dancing it in December. People come from different *tabankas* and, even if they have many other things to do, they put them aside to take part in the dance, especially women and children.

The time varies, as it can be in the afternoon or at night. In this dance, the circle is limited and made up of four people: two boys and two girls who dance around the circle. When one group leaves, another enters, and so on. It's worth noting that each *mandjua* organizes its *Broska* at the same time as the dance. The dangarinos who go to dangle in the other *tabankas* mingle, and only one person wins the dance. In this mingling, there's no one to say that a person is from our *tabanka* or another.

Both *n'ghaies* and *n'kuman* can request this dance. However, all the people taking part in the act are rooting for a person who can attract them. At the time of the *Broska,* if one of the *mandjua* crosses paths with another, they dance against each other, but even if they are from the same *tabanka*, they dance together in order to compete, but if one of them wins, then they say that the *tabanka* won. In fact, not all Brasa organize the *Broska*, particularly those from Patch and Kuntoe do not, with the exception of those who are part of Nhakra.

In *Broska,* the girls, unlike the men, who wear practically nothing to dance, wear cloths on their buttocks, tie their heads back or sideways with lengos and wear coconuts with sleeves on their feet. However, nowadays, i.e. from the year 2000 onwards, they wear whatever clothes they need to dance and instead of tying lengos, they comb their hair. During the *Broska*, and among other groups, the *n'ghaies* perform clowning, among other games, to satisfy people and get them excited about the dance. In the *Broska* dance, giving a person a cloth means that they are being invited to dangle, which they cannot refuse. Nowadays, however, people break these old established rules by refusing to dangle.

On the occasion of the *Broska*, the instrument *Kussunde*[38] is used, which is the name of a viola that was used in the liberation struggle to encourage the soldiers in combat to fight incessantly for the country's independence, by a man whose name was Nfore Sambu, born in the east of the country, mainly in the *tabanka* of Ntchale[39] . Furthermore, in the 1970s and 1980s, N'fore Sambu[40] was considered a pioneer player of the *kussunde* instrument, but he didn't play for the *Broska* dance. Between the early 1990s and the mid-2000s, especially in

[38] *Kussunde* is an instrument made of cabaga, bambo cane stick (this one uses three nylon) and goat leather.
[39] Idem.
[40] Interview given by Bihinha Namara, Sept. 2016.

2002, N'kuia Ura was also considered the best *Broska* player. Unfortunately, he died in 2003 as a result of a long illness. "An hour before the funeral, the big man *(blante binddg*, the circumcised) performed a *Broska* dance in his memory."[41][42] . He was also accused of making a pact with *Irds* about being able to play the *Broska* in order to be exalted throughout the country. It's important to note that Maio Cope was the first artist to sing *Broska* to a wider audience. In addition, Pakual da Kidama and Pakual Fada were renowned *Broska* players. Obviously, they sang it in 1998, the year the civil war began in Guinea-Bissau, when they released their first albums entitled: *junta npadmin*, i.e. military junta is bombing.

Figure 8 - *Kussunde* instrument held by a *n'ghaie*

Source: IBD .[44]

In the early 2000s, the *Kussunde* instrument underwent a slight change in construction when the palm root, which was used as a string, was replaced by nylon thread (three strings/rows) and the number of strings increased. At the same time, the use of *kiseita* was introduced into the *Broska.*

The *Broska* dance, like some others, "[...] is indeed repetitive, but this has no bearing on the ideal impact of the show." (KEALIINOHOMOKU, 2013, p. 131). Subsequently, this dance is also "[...] an ephemeral mode of expression, performed in a form and style determined by the human body moving through space." (KEALIINOHOMOKU, 2013, p. 132).

The *Broska* has the social function of enabling people to live together. It also provides

[41] Interview given by Augusto on September 12, 2016 via Facebook.

[42] Available at: <http://tchogue.blogspot.pt/> . Accessed on: July 20, 2016.

a bond of social cohesion and gratitude to the workers for the work they do, on the one hand, and, on the other, the *Broska* is playful and vital in the lives of young people and aims to strengthen, fraternize and bring harmony between them. It is celebrated to prevent disunity among young people, because disunity has serious consequences, especially betrayal, disillusionment and, above all, the act of revealing the secret of the *tabanka* as a way of destabilizing and/or weakening it.

In front of the *Broska*, the *N'Ghaies* and the other groups of different age groups have the right to wrestle in order to further strengthen the lakes of cohesion, since division leads to mistrust and weakens good coexistence in both the *moransas* and the *tabankas*. Therefore, the young people arrange and organize the *Broska* as a way of avoiding chaos and intrigue in order to be more cohesive. However, the n'gahies are heads of this fight, but if one of the *n'ghaies* doesn't know how to fight well, the *blufu bidag* dismiss him or her so as not to embarrass them, because this fight is where the *tabankas* and *moransas* are classified in order to know whether they have good fighters or not. The *Broska* with another *tabanka* is also meant to strengthen the friendship between the two *tabankas*.

In view of its commemoration, the young people are united and bound together in the face of possible affronts from outsiders. The *Broska* delights young people and it actually strengthens their humanist spirit, which is why they organize it. On the other hand, for the Brasa, this dance makes young people more daring, since through it they begin to face a very large audience and when they are adults they will have no difficulty performing in any place or society. In fact, this dance makes young people more mature in terms of having contacts with people.

5.1 REFLECTIONS ON THE CHANGES AT BROSKA

Before, that is, in the early 1980s to late 1900s, a person couldn't dance *Broska* with shoes on, because they said they wouldn't dance well. However, nowadays people dango with shoes, changing the rules set by the groups that actively participate in *Broska* dancing. Moreover, people used to dance exclusively in the same *tabanka* or *moransa,* but now you can dance *Broska* in one *tabanka* or *moransa* against another and there is no prize for the winners, just like in *Kanta Po.*

In the 1980s and 1990s, it had a lot of impact and recognition among the Brasa, but since the advent of 2000[43] , there has been a big break. This has partly led to a devaluation of this dance, because people, even if they are being called by the talking drum *bumbulum,* don't

[43] Interview granted in Dec. 2015, in Sao Paulo-BA with Guinean immigrants (Brasa).

understand, because they don't know what the sounds mean, because they consider themselves educated and modern people and, in addition, they say that they won't waste their time on these so-called "trivial" things, which is why they don't need to learn *Broska.* As they have moved to the urban center, they have acquired some knowledge there, alienating themselves from the original experience and environment and, considering themselves civilized people, they say they no longer need to dango *Broska*, because according to them, those who dango *Broska* are "uncivilized" and "pre-logical".

These ideas are anchored in the ideological constructions of many people, especially some specialists, for whom, "[...] despite ethnographies [...] proving this fact - that all dangas are ethnic - most Western danga specialists still think they have a certain authority when it comes to the characteristics of 'primitive danga'" (CAMARGO, 2013, p. 18). In these terms, they belittle and devalue other dangas, calling them "primitive". It is clear that these people should no longer maintain the idea that their dangas are pure and authentic and those of others are "primitive", at the risk of people continuing to think that the dangas referred to as "primitive" have no techniques and are performed in an inadequate and incoherent way. In view of this, "it is necessary to insist on the fact that the "primitive danga" form does not exist. Those who teach 'primitive danga' courses are perpetuating a dangerous myth." (KEALIINOHOMOKU, 2013, p. 128).

As Imbali says, "The broska involves practically no expenses." (1992, p. 14). Imbali's studies (1992, p. 14) are partly in line with my ethnographic research. In the *Broska* that is danced in a *tabanka*, the hosts make some preparations, sacrificing pigs, goats and chickens and, above all, they make food for the farmers who have come from another *tabanka* to help them, as a way of thanking them for the hard work they have done, on the one hand, and, on the other, when they go to a *tabanka* or a *moransa* to dance the *Broska*, they have a big party, sacrificing countless animals and making a lot of food for those present.

In the period before the year 2000, chickens and pigs were sacrificed in the *Broska* for those who were going to participate, but nowadays they don't sacrifice anything in the *Broska* that is danced in the same *tabanka or moransa.*In terms of the extent of the dangar and how it is done from one *tabanka* to another, it is obvious that those who go from one *tabanka* to another in order to dangar receive many gifts, such as cane bordao (brandy), red wine, beer, sumo (juice), pork, rice, chicken, but above all money. Then, finally, in the course of this dance there are also people who get very euphoric at having seen some dangarinos dangar so well, and in this sense they give gifts to them.

In this dance, it's also not permissible to go to the *baloba*, which is considered a very sacred place, where they also venerate the Iras and the ancestors, and make an offering to them. But nowadays people go in secret to make their request to Ira in order to win the *Broska,* given the competition and the impact it's having among the Brasa. What's more, dangarinos buy *n'ghol* because it makes the person who possesses it famous in order to win not only the *Broska*, but also the other dangas.

Over time, things are changing and people, instead of *Broska,* sometimes put on *Broska* songs already danced and simply danced to the rhythms of these recorded songs put on the radio. They used to sing live and make a circle for people to dango to, as I did a month ago. Nowadays, on the occasion of the *Broska*, the singers sing while the dancers dango on the same stage, and the spectators, in turn, simply dango to the music.

In recent years, the *Broska* style has been commercialized by musicians who sing the *Broska* in order to praise and praise politicians in exchange for material goods, especially money and cars. On the other hand, they describe the great deeds of both politicians in election campaigns and important people in society, so to speak. This makes a lot of money for their pockets. Because of the interests of the musicians, the *Broska* dance is having another objective, which is commercialization, with the musicians making a profit from the songs they compose in order to give prestige to the politicians to the detriment of the politicians.
to sing for fun in order to strengthen the bonds of friendship and social cohesion between the young people of a particular *tabanka.*

In view of its impact and scope, it should be emphasized that: the Papel are dancing the *Broska*, in this case referring to the Papel from N'dam, those from Biombo and those from Antula Bono, who, in fact, are already quite mixed up with the Brasa. The Mansonka also perform this dance. They dance the *Broska* as if they were Brasa and it, in turn, is spreading and gaining ground among these peoples[44] . In short, the playing of the *Kussunde*, which is now called the *Broska* dance, used to be little practiced but, day after day, it is being considered as a great dance party and is having a significant value among the Brasa people .[45]

[44] Interview given by Sia in July 2015 via video call.
[45] Idem.

6 FINAL CONSIDERATIONS

The focus of this work was to reflect on the changes that have taken place in the Brasa dangas in the face of a scenario marked by constant socio-cultural transformations and their impact on the context of the same society in contemporary times. To this end, the *Broska*, which is a dance created recently, in 1977, is becoming decisive, as is the *Kussunde* in the Brasa milieu; moreover, in the *Broska* style there has been commodification, because the *Broska* is no longer partly celebrated for the amusement of young people, in order to strengthen the lakes of brotherhoods, but is celebrated more to honor people considered important in society, especially politicians. Therefore, the way the musicians are conducting the *Broska*, we can see that the young people are being harmed, because they will probably no longer be interested in pursuing the initial goals of the *Broska*, but rather in commercializing it. Furthermore, it's interesting to note that this dance, unlike the other two discussed in this research, is a popular dance.

The performances of these dangas are a moment of leisure and entertainment for people from different *tabankas*. However, in view of their demands, they have acquired another character, which is that of a dispute, a very strong duel, which allegedly even results in the loss of life of some people, who certainly make a unique pact with the *Iras.* In order to become more popular and famous, the dangarinos secretly go to a fortune-teller in order to win these dangas. Therefore, the elders always interfere using their powers to help the dangarinos of their *tabanka* win both *Kussunde* and *Kanta Po.* In *Kanta Po,* in particular, the elders put their powers into a reliable *blufu bindag*, but the winner is considered to be the leader of a group that attracts the most public and gets more people to follow it, unlike the *Kussunde* dance, where it's the group that wins it. It's obvious that in this dance the symbolic elements that are most at stake are, above all, prestige and bravery.

Roughly speaking, the musicians of *Broska, Kanta Po* and *Kussunde* refer to the difficulties they have experienced both in the *tabanka* and in their personal lives. They also contribute with their songs to the revival of culture, respect for the elderly, appreciation of stable women and their importance in *tabanka*, the exaltation of powerful people in society and the devaluation of marriage today. In addition, they sing to send indirect messages to people who commit adultery in the *tabanka* and those who steal; they sing in reverence of women for their achievements in the *tabanka* and for their values; the latter, in turn, are elated by these songs and welcome them, while the people who have been sent indirect messages are embarrassed and, while some make amends for their nefarious practices, others continue to do so. The *blufu bindag* confess the obscene practices they've done when they're preparing to go to the *fanado,* because if one of them doesn't confess, it's believed that they'll die during their stay in the forest, since the *fanado* for the Brasa is a serious matter, and in the event of a pending slip-up, they'll lose their lives.

"It would be instructive, however, to remember that every danga can change and be developed, even if we find it easier to exclude certain forms as if they had not evolved [...]" (KEALIINOHOMOKU, 2013, p. 128). In the same way, these dangas have undergone some changes in terms of some of the costumes, musical instruments and objects used by dangarinos today, such as the more frequent use of siko in relation to the *bumbulum* and the hiring of *m'beletchu;* moreover, dangarinos dang with shoes instead of without shoes as in the past. Despite receiving new cultural elements, the tradition of this dance remains alive in the face of these transformations. This means that they haven't lost their cultural values, but have become more culturally enriched.

There has been growing prejudice among some Brasa, who have actually decided not to perform this dance, because they consider themselves modern and educated, which is why they no longer perform them. For these people, those who perform these dangas are backward and uncivilized people. Even though these dangas have a great impact on the Brasa, the *Kanta Po* and *Kussunde* dances require a lot of money to be spent on them; in this sense, nowadays, the Brasa often trade in the rice used to support the people who come from different *tabankas* in order to assist them, instead of wasting their savings on the *Kussunde* and *Kanta Po* dances, because the Brasa trade frequently and increasingly than in ancient times. Next, because of its dynamics in terms of disputes and displays of power and demand, *Kanta Po* is usually performed infrequently, because during the preparations for this dance there is always disagreement in the moransas, because a person from one moransa cannot go to another, and if they do, they are considered spies, and sometimes they punish people who dare to go to a rival moransa.

During my ethnographic research, I found that, with regard to the musical instruments, the objects used and the clothing in these dangas, there is more of an addition of other elements from outside than an exchange of these cultural elements for new ones in these dangas. It's worth emphasizing that nowadays there are songs recorded on CDs and videos about these dangas, particularly the *Kussunde* dangas, unlike in ancient times, when there weren't even any records of these dangas.

This research has enabled me to verify that there are not many works written about the cultural identity of the Brasa people, specifically about their dangas. And the results obtained are due to my ethnographic and exploratory research, in being able to bring the cultural values of this people to academia so that anthropologists can take an interest and effectively research their cultural aspects in depth; and also to fill in the theoretical gaps regarding studies of this people in order to demystify the distorted view of them.

It should be noted that there is a shortage of necessary material on this subject, as it is little explored in the academic field. In addition, it can be considered that the results obtained are of great relevance not only in terms of the changes in the objects used, but also in terms of the prejudiced and stereotyped view that some people have of these dangas, since they are labeled "diabolical" and "satanic" by evangelical segments.

Therefore, these dangas should be seen in the context in which they are performed and not in a stereotyped way, drawing hasty illusions with no theoretical basis, but rather from the perspective and belief of the dangarinos, because these dangarinos believe in what they are performing, which is why they give their whole lives and energy to it. Because of this, as Franz Boas says, the dangaras must be seen in the society of which they are a part and not just from the point of view of the observer.

Finally, I am aware that this work may be of benefit to scholars and those curious about the social life of the Brasa and may also enable a deeper and more attentive analysis without preconceived ideas regarding *Kussunde, Kanta Po* and *Broska*, taking into account their social function and their deep structure in order to give more value to the worldview of the Dangarinos and their sympathizers.

REFERENCES

ACOSTA-LEYVA, Pedro. **Africa among Africanists and Africanologists in Brazil**. Belo Horizonte: Virtual Books, 2016.

AUGEL, Moemia Parente. **O Desafio do escombro:** nagao, identidade e pos-colonialismo na literatura da Guine-Bissau. Rio de Janeiro: Garamond, 2007.

BLACKING, John. Movement and meaning: danga from the perspective of Social Anthropology. In: CAMARGO, Giselle Guilhon Antunes (Org.). **Anthropologia da danga I**. Florianopolis: Insular, 2013. p. 75-85.

BUCKLAND, Theresa Jill. Changing perspectives in the ethnography of danga. In: CAMARGO, Giselle Guilhon Antunes (Org.). **Anthropologia da danga I**. Florianopolis: Insular, 2013. p. 143-153.

CAMARGO, Giselle Guilhon Antunes. Anthropology of dance: bibliographical essay. In: CAMARGO, Giselle Guilhon Antunes (Org.). **Antropologia da danga I**. Florianopolis: Insular, 2013. p. 15-29.

CAMMILLERI, Salvatore. **The cultural identity of the Balanta people**. Lisbon: Colibri, 2010.

CARDOSO, Carlos. Ki-yang-yang: a new Balanta religion? **Soronda**. Revista de Estudos Guineenses, Bissau, n. 10, p. 3-15, jul. 1990.

CAVALCANTE, Paulo Sergio Lisboa; JESUS, Aurilene Pereira de. Sabedoria e ancestralidade no Ceara: a didatica dos tambores a sombra da pedagogia do baoba. In: PETIT, Sandra Haydee; SILVA, Geranilde Costa (Orgs.). **Memories of Baoba.** Fortaleza: Edigoes UFC, 2012.

CO, Joao Ribeiro Butiam. **Representation and confinement of social structures in Guinea-Bissau:** an approach to conflicts and consensus. [S.l.: s.n.], 2010.

COUTO, Hildo Honorio do; EMBALO, Filomena. **Literature, language and culture in Guinea-Bissau.** Brasilia: THESAURUS, 2010.

DOMINGOS, Luis Tomas. The African view of nature. **Revista Brasileira de Historia das Religioes**, Maringa, PR, v. 3, n. 9, jan/2011. Available at: <http://www.dhi.uem.br/gtreligiao/pdf8/ST12/003%20-%20Luis%20Tomas%20Domingos.pdf>. Accessed on: September 16, 2016.

FIORIN, Jose Luiz; PETTER, Margarida (Orgs.). **Africa in Brazil:** the formation of the Portuguese language. 2. ed. Sao Paulo: Contexto, 2014.

FORLIN, Marco. **Kussunde, Guinea-Bissau.** 2011. Available at: <https://www.youtube.com/watch?v=xAL3Aoi_BtM>. Accessed on: August 7, 2015.

FORTUNATO, Carlos. **Guine Portal.** 2015. Available at: <http://arteguine.com.sapo.pt/musica.html>. Accessed on: 09 Dec. 2015.

GUINE-BISSAU. **National Institute of Statistics of Guinea-Bissau.** 2015. Available at:<http://www.stat-guinebissau.com/>. Accessed on: September 3, 2016.

HANDEM, Diana. Rice or the balanta brassa identity. **Soronda.** Revista de Estudos Guineenses, Bissau, n. 1, p. 55-67, jul. 1986.

HENRIQUES, Isabel Castro. Colony, colonization, colonial, colonialism. In: SANSONE, Livio; FURTADO, Claudio Alves (Orgs.). **Critical dictionary of the social sciences of Portuguese-speaking countries.** Salvador: EDUFBA, 2014.

HENRIQUES, Isabel Castro. **Colonialism and history.** Lisbon: WP132, 2015.

HERNANDEZ, Leila Leite. **Africa in the classroom**: a visit to contemporary history. 4. ed. Sao Paulo: Selo Negro, 2008.

IMBALI, Faustino. A look at the Balanta food system: the case of the Mato Foroba and Cantone villages. **Soronda.** Journal of Guinean Studies. Bissau, n. 14, p. 03-27, jul. 1992. Available at: <http://www.inepbissau.org/LinkClick.aspx?fileticket=gy19bSoM%2f1M%3d&tabid=61&mid=393>. Accessed on: August 6, 2015.

KAEPPLER, Adrienne L. Danga from an anthropological perspective. In: CAMARGO, Giselle Guilhon Antunes (Org.). **Anthropologia da danga I.** Florianopolis: Insular, 2013. p. 97-121.

KAEPPLER, Adrienne. Danga and the concept of style. In: CAMARGO, Giselle Guilhon Antunes (Org.). **Anthropologia da danga I.** Florianopolis: Insular, 2013. p. 87-96.

KEALIINOHOMOKU, Joann. An anthropologist looks at classical ballet as a form of ethnic dance. In: CAMARGO, Giselle Guilhon Antunes (Org.). **Anthropologia da danga I**. Florianopolis: Insular, 2013. p. 123-142.

KIPP, Eva. **Guinea-Bissau, aspects of the life of a people.** Senegambia, Aug. 19, 2005. Available at: <http://senegambia.blogspot.com.br/2005/08/guin-bissau-aspectos-da-vida-de-um_19.html>. Accessed on: 07 Aug. 2015.

KOUDAWO, Falali; VEIGAS, Caterina Gomes et al. Special issue June 7th. **Soronda.** Journal of Guinean Studies, Bissau, December 2000.

LAU. **Lallalleiro (kussunde)**. 2008. Available at:<http://lallalleiro.blogspot.com.br/2008/06/kusunde.html>. Accessed on: August 7, 2015.

MANE, Fode Abulai. The political-military conflict of June 7th: the crisis of legitimacy. **Soronda.** Revista de Estudos Guineenses, Bissau, p. 67-85, dec. 2000.

MAP OF THE WORLD/Guinea-Bissau map. 2014. Available at: <http://pt.mapsofworld.com/guinea-bissau/>. Accessed on: October 29, 2016.

MENDY, Peter Karibe. Colonial heritage and the challenge of integration. **Soronda.** Revista de Estudos Guineense, Bissau, n. 16, p. 3-37, jul. 1993.

OLIVEIRA, Olavo Borges; HAVIK, Philip J.; SCHIEFER, Ulrich. **Traditional storage in Guinea-Bissau-products, seeds and granaries-Bissau.** Lisbon: Munster, 1996.

PEIXEIRO, Fernando. **Kussunde, the celebration of friends in the shade of the embondeiro tree.** SaposNoticias, May 28, 2012. Available at: <http://noticias.sapo.cv/lusa/artigo/14393339.html>. Accessed on: August 6, 2015.

PEIXEIRO, Fernando. **Canta po, the last feast before circumcision.** SapoNoticias, June 20, 2012. Available at: <http://noticias.sapo.mz/lusa/artigo/14523933.html> Accessed on: 03 May 2016.

RITH, Ttchogue. **Paschal in the Quidama (king of broksa).** 2013. Available at: <https://www.youtube.com/watch?v=NhRyiF0WmuM>. Accessed on: August 7, 2015.

RITH, Ttchogue. FREHU-N-FLIF N° 13: family composition in Balanta culture. **Balanta Intellectuals in the Diaspora**. Oslo, no. 13, June 2013. Available at: <http://tchogue.blogspot.com.br/2013/06/frehu-n-flif-n-13-composicao-da-familia.html> Accessed: June 26, 2015.

SEIBERT, Gerhard. Creolization in Cape Verde and Sao Tome and Principe: historical and identity divergences. **Afro-Asia**. Salvador, n. 49, p. 41-70, 2014.

SIGA, Fernando. **The social, political and religious organization of the Balanta:** uses, customs and rituals. 2015. 68 f Monograph (Bachelor in Humanities) - University of International Integration of Afro-Brazilian Lusophony, Redengao, 2015.

SILVA, Francisco Henriques da; SANTOS, Mario Beja. **From Guinea-Portuguese to Guinea-Bissau:** a roadmap. Porto: Fronteira do Caos Editores, 2014.

SIMOES, Landerset. **Babel negra:** etnografia, arte e cultura dos indigenas da Guine Porto: O COMERCIO DO PORTO, [1935?].

YOUNGERMAN, Suzanne. Curt Sanchs and his heranga: a critical review of the world history of danga with a survey of recent studies that perpetuate his ideas. In: CAMARGO, Giselle Guilhon Antunes (Org.). **Antropologia da danga I**. Florianopolis: Insular, 2013. p. 57-74.

ZEMP, Hugo. To enter the dance. In: CAMARGO, Giselle Guilhon Antunes (Org.). **Anthropologia da danga I.** Florianopolis: Insular, 2013. p. 31-56.

ZURARA, Gomes Eanes de. **Cronica do descobrimento e conquista da Guine.** Sintra: Francisco Lyon de Castro, [1948?].

GLOSSARY

Animism: Traditional religion in which elements of nature are endowed with divine powers. It is often used pejoratively to inferiorize African cults.

Baloba: Sacred place where petitions, offerings and prayers are made.

Fanado: Ritual of sexual initiation (genital circumcision) for both sexes; in this work, the term applies only to men.

Fram: Sacred place of *Buule* (the Ember God) where prayers and offerings are made. It is worth emphasizing *that* Fram also enables vital energy.

Fo n'ghol: A bird whose head is used in a traditional ritual performed by soothsayers to give powers to anyone.

Wrath: A supreme being.

Kata: A kind of traditional skirt; it's made from different pieces of comb cloth in different colors.

Kiseita: Sound clapper. An instrument made from milk cans; sometimes made from beer caps. These are also usually bent by piercing them. Then wire is used to hold them together so that they can be worn on the feet. Finally, pebbles are inserted to extract sounds. Once the instrument has been built, it is tied to the foot and then the dangarino moves to extract the sound from the instrument.

Lope: Cloth folded in the shape of a calgao, used in some dangas and various manifestations.

Mandjua: Group of people identified by belonging to the same age group.

M'beletchu: wooden leg. A person who augments their feet with sticks in order to make them longer. They wear red clothes that cover their entire body. Generally speaking, some Muslims dress as such. The m'beletchus charm people who contribute money. They also come out at Carnival, especially at Muslim cultural events.

Moransa: "[...] is a group of houses belonging to the same large family, which share a single paternal grandfather [...]" (RITH, 2013, p. 1). In addition, "The *houses* are also built according to the location of the family rice field." (HANDEM, 1986, p. 64-65).

N'faia: Skirt traditionally made by the dangarinos themselves and worn commonly in dangas. This skirt is made from cabaceira bark and malila.

Siko: Musical instrument commonly used in various cultural manifestations in GuiiK'-Bissau. Recently, it has been incorporated into the dangas described in this work as a new element. The Siko is a kind of small, light drum, played to extract the softest, most pleasant sound.

Tabanka: (Village) "[...] is made up of a group of several unique families whose link consists of having a common ancestry" (RITH, 2013, p. 1).

Bumbulum: A talking drum used to communicate various messages, which also serves as a musical instrument.

Printed by Books on Demand GmbH, Norderstedt / Germany